Color Guide to
TROPICAL FISH

By HERBERT R. AXELROD and WILLIAM VORDERWINKLER

 STERLING PUBLISHING CO., INC.   NEW YORK

The Oak Tree Press LONDON AND SYDNEY

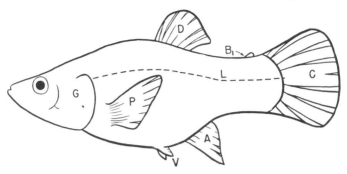

D—DORSAL FIN; C—CAUDAL FIN; P—PECTORAL FIN; G—GILL COVER;
A—ANAL FIN; V—VENTRAL FINS; L—LATERAL LINE; B₁—ADIPOSE FIN

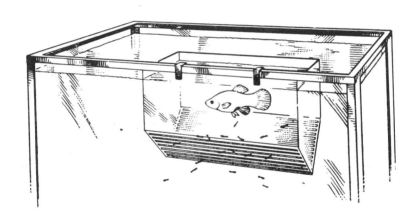

Sixth Printing, 1969
Copyright © 1968, 1959, 1955 by
Sterling Publishing Co., Inc.
419 Park Avenue South, New York 10016
British edition published in Great Britain and the Commonwealth by
The Oak Tree Press, Ltd., 116 Baker St., London, W.1.
Manufactured in the United States of America
All rights reserved
Standard Book Number 8069-3704-1
UK 7061 2128 7   8069-3705-X

HOW TO USE THIS COLOR GUIDE

Actual count shows that there have been 67 books on tropical fishes published since 1900. Most of them list the various fishes in evolutionary order, by their family characteristics. A few others list the fishes in alphabetical order. But all of these books require a prior knowledge of tropical fishes (their breeding habits, their relative size or their shape) before a specific fish can be found in the pages by name.

This book is different! It has been arranged according to the color and color pattern of the fish. Certainly it is easier to identify and remember a fish this way than by his long and mysterious scientific name.

To make matters simple, this guide is divided into these color categories:

Fishes with horizontal stripes.

Fishes with vertical stripes.

Fishes whose predominant color is red.
Included in this section are fishes of yellow, gold, and brown because a red fish might, in some environmental situations, assume any or all of these related colors.

Fishes with a basically blue coloration.
Green, silver, and black fishes may be found here since they, too, may vary in shadings.

This method of color division makes reference to a particular fish very simple. Then once you know the scientific name of a fish, you can consult the index in the back of the book for later reference.

You'll also find a glossary in the back of the book to give you the exact meanings of the family names, technical and semi-technical terms commonly used in "tropical fish language" plus descriptions in detail of the breeding habits sometimes referred to on the various text pages.

This system, unique as it is, raises several minor questions. First, how can we classify fishes who have more than one basic color pattern (like *Neolebias ansorgei,* who is both red and blue)? . . . Or a fish who is vertically striped and blue at the same time (like *Epiplatys sexfasciatus*)? . . . Or a fish with both red and blue and striped both vertically and horizontally (like *Crenicara maculata*)? The solution is this: we've illustrated these fishes in color right here at the start, because they are, fortunately, the exception rather than the rule.

Our only other problem is with Guppies! Guppies may be obtained in any color, any color pattern, any size, shape or form. What did we do with these? We put them in the last section (on pages 120, 121, and 125), because in the wild they are basically silver!

If you are beginning an aquarium or adding to one, you can select from the pictures here the color fishes which are most pleasing to you. Remember, when you select your fishes, to choose according to size as well as color pattern because the old saying (with a new twist) still holds: "Big fishes eat little fishes, regardless of color."

Crenicara maculata

(Below) Known as "Checkerboard Cichlid," this is a handsome fish. We have seen males about 4 inches long; females are smaller with more distinct markings, but their colors cannot compete with the splendor of the male. Parents take good care of their brood, but broods seem to be few and far between.

Neolebias ansorgei

(Above) This timid little fellow comes to us from the western part of Africa. He makes up in color for his diminutive proportions. Best kept alone in well-planted aquaria.

Epiplatys sexfasciatus

A timid fish who likes a well-shaded aquarium, preferably with broad-leaved plants to hover under. (Also see page 36.)

Corydoras arcuatus

Down South America way, in muddy side streams and slow moving rivers, a pretty little Catfish can be noticed stirring up the muck on the bottom of the water. Always searching for bits of food passed up by fishes inhabiting the upper strata of water, the popular *Corydoras arcuatus,* affectionately known as "The Skunk Catfish" because of the skunk-like stripe running along his back, is a useful scavenger in the home aquarium.

He is particularly useful when an aquarium full of Zebrafish is being maintained, for the Zebra likes to stay at the surface of the water where his peculiarly adapted mouth, which opens at the top, can easily catch any small insects which fall on the surface. Often the Zebrafish will ignore particles which fall on the bottom, and since uneaten food fouls the water, a scavenger must be employed to tackle the housecleaning job.

Brachydanio rerio

The Zebrafish, scientifically known as *Brachydanio rerio,* is somewhat of a misnomer, for the stripes are horizontal and not vertical as on the four-legged Zebra.

The Zebrafish, originally from Bengal, India, is so easily bred that imported fish are rare. The same with the Spotted Danio; why should they be brought from India when they can be raised by the millions in Florida?

Both the Zebrafish and the Spotted Danio are peaceful and extremely hardy, two features which make them valuable additions to any aquarium collection. They breed by scattering eggs haphazardly among fairly dense vegetation. Unless the breeders are removed after spawning they will make a meal of their spawn. Males and females look very much alike and only the plump belly of the female is any clue at all. It is possible to interbreed among some fishes of the genus *Brachydanio.*

Brachydanio nigrofasciatus (on left page, bottom)

Known as the Spotted Danio, this fish is the closest relative of the *B. rerio* shown on the top of this page.

Rasbora steineri

The *Rasbora* genus is a large one. All those members of this family with which we are acquainted have proven to be excellent aquarium fishes, and the *R. steineri* (first known as *Rasbora cambodia*) is no exception. These peaceful, small fish are not so timid as to be hidden all the time, and not so bold that they pick on other fishes.

So far, there has been only one shipment of this fish into the United States, and it came into California from Cambodia, Indo-China.

Breeding attempts have failed so far as we know, and this attractive fish is still a challenge to the skill and ingenuity of the amateur as well as the professional breeder.

Apistogramma U3

For a long time this fish has been very popular among aquarists. He was known to be a species of *Apistogramma*, but nobody seemed to know which. It was finally decided to call him *Apistogramma* U3, the "U" standing for "unbekannt" or "unknown."

The picture speaks for itself; it might be added that the female illustrated here is a bit small. The male, of course, has the brighter colors, the bigger fins, and the bossy disposition (which he promptly loses when spawning is completed). His habitat is in the South American country of Surinam (Dutch Guiana), in the neighborhood of Paramaribo. These fish are easily kept, and will spawn readily if given a preponderance of living foods in their diet.

Corydoras leopardus

Something about the Catfishes appeals to a great number of aquarists. This one has been known to science since 1906, and has achieved a lot of recent popularity.

These fish do a wonderful job of devouring food passed up by the other fishes, thereby preventing a fouled tank. Catfish spend practically all their time on the bottom, busily poking in the gravel for anything fit to eat. Their poking, however, is done gently enough so that hardly ever is a well-rooted plant dug up.

Sexing a mature pair of fish is usually simple with the *Corydoras* species. Looked at from above, the female has a considerably wider body. This is much more reliable than the usually recommended method of looking for the more pointed fins in the male. The well-marked dorsal fin of the male is not always easily distinguishable.

Hemigrammus gracilis

This fish is popularly known as the Glow-Light Tetra, and for very good reason. With lighting from above in a well-planted tank, the fish appears to have a red neon tube running through him. A school of these lovely fish in the proper surroundings is a sight to make even a hard-boiled aquarist gasp.

This fish is often passed up when seen in a dealer's bare tank. The otherwise bright red streak might then be a pale yellow, scarcely noticeable.

The *Hemigrammus* is happiest in soft, slightly acid water. He is shy, but gets along well with other fishes, and is a desirable addition to any community tank. However, he is one of the more difficult species to breed, probably because aquarists do not take enough pains to make sure he has the proper conditions. He has been known to science since 1874, and is native to the upper reaches of the Amazon River.

Cubanichthys cubensis

"The Cuban fish from Cuba." This popular fellow is not fond of dried food. Breeding is like few other fishes: the female expels the eggs in a bunch, and they hang from her vent like a bunch of grapes on a string. The male fertilizes them, and the eggs hang there until brushed off onto a plant.

Apistogramma agassizi

Why the *Apistogramma agassizi* is not more popular among American aquarists is a mystery. He is peaceful enough to be classified as a community fish. Also, as the illustration clearly shows, he does not lack beauty.

Native to the middle regions of the Amazon, this fish is found in quite a wide area. As is usual, the male is the larger, more brightly colored specimen, in this case the upper one.

Where most Cichlids usually choose a rock for spawning, the *A. agassizi* has been known to use a broad plant leaf at times. One of the editors recalls acquiring a pair when they first arrived in New York (circa 1932), for the then steep price of five dollars. They spawned seven times, and each time the female promptly ate the eggs. When the female died, there were none available to replace her.

Spawning is not really so difficult. The important thing is to use a healthy, well-conditioned pair. (This is good advice when breeding any fish.)

← Hemigrammus pulcher (on left page, bottom)

Rather heavy-bodied, the *H. pulcher* reminds us of the *Rasbora heteromorpha*.

Peaceful and easily fed, he comes from the Peruvian Amazon. Sexes are not always easy to distinguish; the lower one is the female.

Puntius lineatus

This fish is said to be the same as *Puntius fasciatus,* shown on page 25. A close look at both pictures will easily show you that they are considerably different, both in body form and in colors. This is a silvery fish, not greenish-gold like the other.

The proper naming of fishes becomes more and more complicated as we penetrate further and further into previously unexplored streams and find more aquarium fishes for the hobbyist. New roads are always being built, and the airlines are constantly adding service to previously inaccessible locations. Fish collectors are ever on the alert for new and colorful species in these new places, and the taxonomist's job becomes increasingly more complicated.

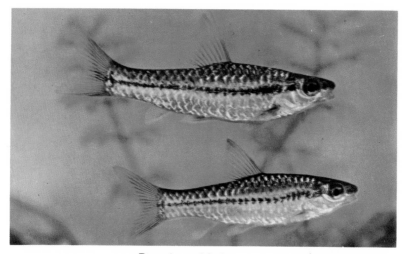

Puntius ablabes

(Above) Most of our Barbs come to us from the Far East, but a considerable number are turning up lately from Africa as well. Such is the case with the fish on this page. The *Puntius ablabes* has a very attractive, iridescent sparkle to its scales which our illustration only hints at.

Puntius chlorotaenia

(Below) The *Puntius chlorotaenia* is another African Barb with which we have only recently become familiar. The pair shown here is still slightly immature. The female (lower fish) later became much bigger and fuller in girth, and the pair spawned readily.

Otocinclus arnoldi

The little *Otocinclus arnoldi* does a real service for the aquarist. He is always busy, poking around behind rocks and on the gravel for uneaten food. When he is not doing this, he nibbles algae from the plants, glass and rocks.

The control of algae is important in a well-lighted aquarium, and a few of these little fellows will make a big difference in the overall appearance of your aquarium. Snails are credited with controlling algae; however, we find that a snail is often carried away with enthusiasm and not only eats algae but eats holes in the plant too, a habit an *Otocinclus* will not be found guilty of.

This is one of the fishes which must occasionally come to the surface for a gulp of air. He generally blends in fairly well with his background, and in a heavily planted tank is sometimes very difficult to find.

He is said to come from flowing waters, where his sucking mouth is useful for anchoring himself against the current on rocks.

Hyphessobrycon innesi

Here we have what is undoubtedly the king of small aquarium fishes, the famous Neon Tetra. He is probably the only fish ever shipped overseas by dirigible.

In 1936, a Frenchman named Rabaut traveled far up the Amazon in search of rare butterflies and orchids. Upon finding these lovely fish in the jungle creeks of this region, he promptly became a fish collector instead. He brought some back to Paris with him, and these were promptly put aboard the dirigible "Hindenburg" and sent to Dr. W. T. Innes in Philadelphia.

They withstood almost freezing temperatures on the way, came through the ordeal alive, and promptly caused a furor among aquarists who saw them. They were named for Dr. Innes by Dr. George S. Myers, an old friend of his.

Getting these beauties to spawn was a puzzle for quite a while. It was found that aquarists in some parts of Germany had little or no trouble, and others found it impossible. Now they are bred by the thousands . . . the secret is in the water.

Aplocheilus lineatus

This colorful fish, one of our larger "Panchaxes," comes to us from India. His bright colors, which never fail to attract attention, make him a favorite in his family.

He is a talented jumper, and a covered aquarium is a necessity. He is not man-eating but prefers living foods, especially mosquito larvae or small fishes. In his native country, his healthy appetite probably accounts for the untimely demise of many mosquitoes and other water insects. He has the knack of drifting gently up to his intended victim until he is close by, and then with a lightning-like sidewards thrust, he devours his prey.

Don't keep this fellow with small fishes, unless you intend them for his food. He can conquer a fair-sized Neon Tetra, as we found out when Neons were still expensive.

This fish was identified by Valenciennes as far back as 1846, and has been popular among aquarists for many a year. They breed easily, and the young are easily raised.

Acestrorhynhcus cachorro

It is very easy to see why this fellow will never win a popularity contest among aquarists. Just take a look at his dental equipment! Collectors say that in some regions it is difficult to pull a seine without getting a few of these devils in among the catch, gorging themselves on the captured fish until they seem about to burst. They are difficult to keep, too. For all their roughneck tactics, their scales damage easily when they are caught, and they usually die soon afterward.

Rasbora urophthalmus

One of the latest additions to this familiar genus of aquarium fishes is *Rasbora urophthalmus*. He was first imported to the United States in 1955 and this is the first illustration ever to appear in print.

The feeding habits of this fish are very encouraging, and though they show a favoritism for the live foods (such as Daphnia and Tubifex), they get along very well on ordinary dried foods.

Attempts are being made to breed this fish and some success has been reached when soft, acid water is used. These *Rasbora* spawn by laying adhesive eggs on the leaves of plants, and they seem to prefer *Cryptocoryne* plants for some reason.

The males can be differentiated from the females by their comparatively slender appearance.

Hyphessobrycon metae

All too seldom is this South American beauty found in dealers' tanks.

This is a shy fish, and a shy fish should not be put in a tank which adds to his shyness. Placing this fish in a brightly lighted, sparsely planted tank will not put him at his ease, and certainly will not encourage him to spawn. It must be remembered that he comes from heavily shaded jungle streams, where there is seldom any sunlight.

In a well-planted aquarium there would be plenty of dark, shaded nooks where this "Tetra Loretto" can hide if danger threatens. In this environment there is no timidity on the part of the fish at all. Putting him into a completely shaded aquarium would not permit us to admire him so a happy medium would be a tank well planted on one end.

There is no record of this fish having spawned in captivity as yet.

Cheirodon axelrodi

The Cardinal Tetra, as this fish was called upon its recent introduction, caused quite an uproar in the scientific world when it came time to name it. Almost simultaneously it was named *Hyphessobrycon cardinalis* and *Cheirodon axelrodi*; when it was finally decided that it belonged to the genus *Cheirodon,* the name which honored one of the editors of this work was officially assigned to it. Some German works still stubbornly refer to it by its incorrect name.

The fish is just as beautiful as its picture indicates. In size it slightly exceeds the Neon Tetra, which it resembles except for a much greater amount of red in the body. The Cardinal Tetra is as peaceful as it is gorgeous—a perfect aquarium fish.

Epalzeorhynchus kalopterus (on right page, bottom) —

Although this fish resembles the *Anostomus,* he comes from a totally different part of the world: the East Indies. A peaceful fish, he is inclined to spend much of his time at or near the bottom. The popular name "Pal" has been suggested to replace the tongue-twisting scientific name of this recently-introduced fish.

Anostomus anostomus

(Above) This Amazonian fish with a double-barreled name has alternating dark brown and golden stripes and deep red fins. He grows to a length of approximately five inches and is a beauty, but not recommended for small aquaria. Spawnings are occasionally reported.

Rasbora pauciperforata

This fish is one of the newer introductions of the popular genus *Rasbora*. His general body pattern is shared by some of the other *Rasbora* (such as *R. lateristriata* and *R. meinkeni*). All come from the Malay Peninsula and Indonesia, and are peaceful and easily kept in aquaria. They eat prepared as well as live foods, and observe the "good neighbor" policy.

This species is distinguished by his bright red lateral line, which appears as bright as the illustration only when conditions are right. The female may be distinguished by her fuller, deeper body; she appears at the top in this illustration.

To keep these lovely fish in good spirits keep them in a group. In their native habitat, they usually are found in large schools, and a fish of this disposition is sure to be very unhappy if kept singly or in pairs.

We have not heard of *R. pauciperforata* being bred, at least not in the United States.

Puntius fasciatus

This is the Striped Barb, who would be one of our most popular aquarium fishes, if only the supply were more plentiful.

One very skillful breeder, Fred Corwin, has had them spawn for him several times, but in each case the fry seemed to be delicate and difficult to raise. In contrast to this, the fish is said to be very common in his native clear river waters of Singapore, Malacca, Thailand, Sumatra, Java and Borneo. He has been known to science since 1853, but aquarists did not get to see him until about 1935. This is a fish it might pay the experienced aquarist to attempt propagating.

His horizontal dark stripes on a golden background make a very pleasing pattern, and the fish does not have (nor need) any other colors. He is peaceful, and those who are fortunate enough to own a Striped Barb are usually very proud of him.

In captivity he may attain a length of about four inches, but in his native state he has been known to double this size.

Xiphophorus helleri

At some time or other most hobbyists have seen the Mexican Sword-tail. The editors remember him as the first tropical fish they had ever seen. This was about 35 years ago, in Rabenau's establishment in Brooklyn. At the time it was very expensive to collect beyond the Goldfish stage. The fact that Swordtails are still among the prime favorites of aquarium fishes is certainly proof that they have plenty of appeal.

What makes them popular with beginners is that they are one of a group who bear their young alive. What is more, the young fish have a good appetite and are easily raised. Many advanced aquarists even breed them with the intention of establishing color strains, most of which are a great improvement over the original fish. They also cross-breed easily with other species, and some interesting hybrids are produced in this manner. Contrary to the *Danio* hybrids, most of the *Xiphophorus* hybrids are fertile, and all sorts of interesting combinations are possible.

Tanichthys albonubes

(Above) The White Cloud Mountain Fish from China was an exciting introduction when aquarists in this country first saw it in the early '30s. Pretty, easily bred, requiring little space, it is one of our hardiest aquarium fishes. Aquarists the world over accepted it as one of their favorites, and it still enjoys a very high popularity.

(Below) Never consider anything impossible where fish-breeding is concerned! The "Meteor Minnow" has been developed from the short-finned variety of the fish shown above, and we predict that further selective breeding will result in veil-tailed specimens like our present-day fancy Guppies. All right, fish-breeders, let's see what you can do!

Nannostomus trifasciatus

The colors in the picture give you a good idea of the beautiful iridescent quality of the fish's coloring. In order to get the proper view of this iridescence, your light must be properly placed, not behind the fish, but in front.

Here is an illustration of how one can be fooled if the sex of a fish is judged by body form alone. The upper fish in the picture seems to be the female as it has the heavier body. But look at its bright red fins, compared with the less bright fins of the one below, and you see that the top fish is the male.

Judging sex of some fishes takes a bit of experience. The editors once took two Zebra Danios to a monthly competition, strictly as a joke. Both were females, one nicely rounded with eggs, and the other quite slim, having recently spawned. Amazingly enough, they passed for a pair and took the blue ribbon!

Nannostomus marginatus

This is the largest, most beautiful, and most difficult to breed of the *Nannostomus* species.

The best way to look at this fish is to place him in a well-planted aquarium with a dark background and have the light come in from over the observer's shoulder. This brings out not only the colors of the fish's pigmentation, but the many reflected colors which would not otherwise be visible. Many of our fishes which look only silvery under normal light gleam in mother-of-pearl tints when we let the light strike them from behind the observer.

We see the same effect when we look at a diamond. If we look through it, it resembles a piece of glass, but if we let it reflect light, it becomes the beautiful thing it was intended to be. A smart aquarist who wants his aquarium to be a thing of beauty experiments with his lighting, and sometimes gets a great deal of beauty out of a group of fishes which would otherwise look nondescript.

Nannostomus beckfordi

This fish was long known to aquarists as *Nannostomus anomalus* but it is recognized now as a new species.

Ichthyologists identify a fish scientifically by a very complicated procedure which entails counting scales, fin-rays, teeth, etc. When all this is done and the fish scientist announces what he firmly believes to be a new fish, it often happens that an old publication turns up with the same fish pictured or listed. Or, conversely, as in this case, a similarity of features indicates that two fishes are exactly alike when it is found that one differs in some small way and is really a new fish.

The *N. beckfordi* is about the same size as the *N. trifasciatus,* and has proven to be by far the easier of the two to breed. In a sunny, well-planted aquarium the red in the body line and fins has a lovely gleam which is not otherwise appreciated. Here, as usual, you can notice no great difference in body depth, but the upper fish may be distinguished as the male by his deeper colors and higher dorsal fin.

Ophiocephalus senegalus

We do not as yet see many of these fish in the United States, and they are barely mentioned in any of the published works we have at hand. This seems to be one of the larger species, and also one of the "tough customers."

A close relative, the *Channa asiatica,* is an outstanding example of toughness. Fish dealers in the Orient carry both these fishes around in baskets, packed in wet grass. When a customer wants a piece of fish, he cuts off the piece required and plops the rest back. The top half of the fish goes on living for hours.

Thayeria obliqua

When the British speak of "Penguins" in their aquaria, they are not referring to the odd birds from the Antarctic. They mean the *Thayeria obliqua*.

The position in which we see them in the picture is not an unusual angle. They are very active, and are usually to be found in front without much searching. Although not highly colored, the deep black stripe which extends from the gill-covers all the way down through the lower caudal lobe makes a striking contrast to the silvery belly, and does give these fish a penguin-like appearance.

Sexes vary little in color, but the heavier body of the female, in this case the upper fish, is our only means of differentiation.

The Penguin Fish comes from the Amazon, in the vicinity of Obidos, and, although not seen in the United States until less than 10 years ago, they have been known to science since 1908. The European breeders have stolen a march with this fish; most of the tank-bred fish of this species come to us from Germany. Fortunately the supply is good if not plentiful.

Cichlasoma facetum

The granddaddy of all aquarium-kept Cichlids is the *Cichlasoma facetum,* popularly named the "Chanchito." It is therefore fitting that we begin this section of vertically striped fishes by introducing this one.

Known to aquarists since 1889, specimens are seen everywhere. They are a bit big for the average aquaria, and their habits include a very unpleasing one of tearing up plants. This action is an instinctive one, and its purpose is to create an open space where enemies cannot make a sneak attack.

Colors vary with chameleon-like rapidity, depending upon the background. These fish are devoted parents, guarding the eggs and fry constantly. They make interesting pets, if their quarters are roomy enough.

This is one of the "surprise" fishes which can be bought when one or two inches in length; they grow and grow until they attain a length of 6 to 8 inches. When buying these fish, find out if they are full-grown and if not, find out how big they will be when they are full-grown.

Monodactylus argenteus

(Above) The "Mono" is found mostly in salt waters along the eastern coast of Africa to Australia. It often ascends rivers into brackish and fresh water, and is therefore one of those rare species which can be kept in marine aquaria as well as those containing fresh water, providing the change is not too sudden.

Puntius nigrofasciatus

(Below) This beautiful member of the Barb family from Ceylon undergoes a real transformation at breeding time. Usually he is rather nondescript. When breeding time arrives, however, the male's grayish silvery background turns into a deep ruby-red and his bars become deep black.

Cichlasoma severum

The *Cichlasoma severum's* vertical stripes appear only in young specimens. As the fish grows older, his stripes gradually disappear, and when he is full-grown there is only one left, the dark one near the tail.

He is also quite a large fish when full-grown, attaining a length of eight inches or thereabouts. At this time the body takes on a greenish tinge, and the male becomes peppered with red dots.

As with the Chanchito, you need a large aquarium for these fish, and if you intend to breed them, be prepared to house from 500 to as many as 1000 youngsters.

In appearance the young greatly resemble the young of *Symphysodon discus* (see page 49). There have been cases where they were sold as such, causing great consternation among dealers and customers who bought what they honestly believed to be *Symphysodon discus,* and paid many times what *C. severum* were worth.

Epiplatys sexfasciatus

How to classify this fish (for this book) by his body markings presented quite a problem: the female has vertical bars, and the male has horizontal rows of dots! Because the female has the more pronounced markings, the stripes won out. Mother Nature has been stingy with her as far as other colors are concerned, however.

This is one of the larger members of the *Panchax* group, and is better kept away from smaller fishes. Contrary to the temperament of most other *Panchax,* this is a shy fish. His tank should be well-planted, especially with wide-leaved plants, such as *Cryptocoryne willisii* or Amazon Swordplants. He has a great time scooting among the stems and hiding under the broad leaves.

This fish is native to the west coast of Africa, from Liberia to the Congo. He can be bred with regularity.

Botia strigata

We have here a species of *Botia* which has just arrived in the United States. This genus is restricted in habitat to Thailand, Malacca, Singapore, Java, Sumatra and Borneo.

Chances are not very great that this fish will achieve a real measure of popularity, except as a rarity. He does not seem to be as highly colored as the rest of his family, and unfortunately seems to be a fish with nocturnal habits. He spends most of the daylight hours in hiding.

In appearance he resembles the Weather-fish which is native to Europe and parts of Asia, and is popular among European aquarists. Some hobbyists keep Weather-fish more or less as a barometer. When there is a thunderstorm coming up, they become very active; so active in fact that they stir up the bottom! Whether the *Botia* shown here also has this characteristic we do not know, but the two are related.

Monodactylus sebae

On his collecting trip to West Africa in 1957, Herbert R. Axelrod captured a number of these beauties, among them the fish shown here. They are difficult to catch, and even harder to keep alive. Like the *Monodactylus argenteus,* we know nothing of their breeding habits and it is quite possible that spawning is accomplished in marine waters.

These fish are hard to handle because they bruise easily, become infected and subsequently die. Fully grown wild specimens are quite large, but if we are ever fortunate to grow some of them in aquaria, they will undoubtedly be considerably smaller. The specimens shown here were collected in the Wouri River, Cameroon.

Aphyosemion coeruleum

One of the real aristocrats of the aquarium is the Blue Gularis, as the *Aphyosemion coeruleum* is generally called. You might classify him as having horizontal as well as vertical stripes. There are a few more vertical stripes, however.

The male's background color is blue. His stripes are maroon, and the area between the middle and lower prongs of his three-pronged tail fin is the real feature: bright orange. It seems that the female was hiding behind the door when colors were being passed out; she has practically none.

Breeding these fish is a rather painstaking procedure, and they are therefore not often available to aquarists. They have a huge appetite, and become tame enough to take food from your fingers.

Puntius semifasciolatus

China does not give us many species of aquarium fishes, but this is one. Native to southeastern China, this fish has been known to aquarists for a long time.

The pair shown here are immature; if they were full-grown, you would notice that the male is considerably smaller than the female. He may also be identified by his slimmer proportions.

Unless these fish are in the best of condition, the red in their fins does not show with nearly as great intensity as pictured here.

This fish is peaceful, goes about his own business without ever annoying any of his neighbors, and because of this may be considered a perfect candidate for the community aquarium.

The popular name for this fish is "The Half-banded Barb." He attains a length of about 2½ inches in the aquarium and is very hardy.

Puntius sachsi

A bright golden fish makes a beautiful contrast against the green of a well-planted aquarium. Here we have one which fills the bill perfectly.

Until very recently this fish was believed to be a golden "sport" of the *P. semifasciolatus*. This fish was introduced some years ago by a breeder in New Jersey named Schubert, and was long called *Barbus schuberti* in his honor. The fish achieved a great deal of popularity under this name, and aquarists dislike giving up a name they have gotten used to. However, he has been positively identified now as *Puntius sachsi*.

Here again the male is the smaller fish, and the black markings on the sides vary greatly. As can be seen, there are only suggestions of markings on the female. These are just as peaceful and satisfactory as the *P. semifasciolatus* (see opposite page) in every way.

Abramites microcephalus

This fish is one of the oddities which comes to us from the Amazon region in South America. It is one of the larger members of the Tetra family, and like the *Chilodus punctatus* (page 103) swims with its head tilted downward. This species is fond of poking along the bottom on the lookout for any food which may have fallen there, and is also fond of a diet which includes some vegetable matter like algae, which is often picked off the plants. They are peaceful toward other tankmates, and have been known to live a long time, once they have become well established in an aquarium.

We have heard of only one spawning; all the eggs but one became fungussed, but that one hatched and was raised to maturity.

Macropodus opercularis

What was the first tropical fish known to aquarists? That's an easy one to answer; it was the Paradise Fish, shown here. He was introduced to European aquarists in the year 1869, and is still available today.

We have many such Labyrinth Fishes now, but imagine the joy among the aquarists of that day when they first found out that these fish are not only beautiful, but have many interesting habits:

they build a nest of bubbles, in which they keep their eggs;

they don't eat their eggs as a Goldfish does, but guard them faithfully until the young are able to shift for themselves;

they actually drown if they cannot come to the surface for an occasional gulp of air.

All these interesting habits and their graceful streamlining made them precious things indeed, well worth the difficulties encountered in those days of 1869 when there arose the problem of heating an aquarium properly and evenly.

Mesogonistius chaetodon

This fish, known as the Black-Banded Sunfish, like a prophet, is without honor in his home land (New Jersey to Georgia). A beautiful fish, he is prized by aquarists in foreign countries, and practically unheard of here.

He has a vicious temperament and warrants his own aquarium.

In breeding, the male, in true Cichlid fashion, shows extreme devotion to his fry. The female is not very attentive, but drives the male back if he tries to leave the nesting area.

Puntius tetrazonus

The most popular of all Barbs (so called because this fish is incorrectly known as belonging to the genus *Barbus*) is this *Puntius tetrazonus*. This beautiful animal has been known under many incorrect names including *Barbus sumatranus,* a name still used in some places. Several popular names have been awarded this fish; some prefer Tiger Barbs, and others "Sumatranus."

So easy is it to spawn these fish, that imported specimens haven't been seen for many years. They breed by scattering semi-adhesive eggs into very heavy plant clumps. Breeders should be removed immediately after spawning or they will devour their own eggs. The young hatch in a few days at 76°F., and that temperature is ideal for them.

Pterophyllum eimekei

There is probably no fish with more dignified bearing than this one, the Angelfish. His habitats are the Peruvian and Ecuadorian sections of the Amazon, and also the Essequibo River. First brought into captivity in 1911, he has been one of the perennial favorites.

Here is a fish who will attract immediate attention from anyone. It is interesting to watch someone getting his first look at your aquaria, and watch him gravitate toward the Angelfish; no matter what else you may have, he will generally ask what the Angelfish are, and tell you how beautiful they look. They get large, so don't skimp on the tank space you allow for them.

At first, aquarists had a difficult time getting Angelfish to spawn, but succeeding generations of the fish have acclimated themselves to aquaria life so well that now it is possible for almost anyone with a well-conditioned pair to get them to spawn, if he knows how. The spawning act is so interesting that every aquarist should witness it at least once.

Tilapia melanopleura

From the Congo region of Africa comes this beautiful member of the family of fishes with the strange habit of caring for their eggs and young by carrying them around in the mouth. This species is identified by a bright red in the belly region, which becomes especially brilliant when spawning time approaches. The eggs are picked up by one of the parents, usually the female, after they have been laid and fertilized, and then she swims around for about two weeks without touching food, her mouth and throat distended with the eggs. It has been proven that these eggs will not hatch unless they are in the parent's mouth. There must be a secretion which is necessary to the proper development of the eggs in the fish's mouth.

Acanthophthalmus semicinctus

The tongue-twisting name *Acanthophthalmus* actually means "Thorn-eye." The reason for the name is that the fish of this genus are provided with a strange, thorn-shaped ray just below the eye. It probably was once used for protection, because the fish can make the ray stick out at right angles if he so desires. However, we have not heard of his using it on other fish, and therefore consider him a useful community fish.

This interesting little fellow is quite nicely colored and makes a desirable addition to any collection. He is also useful as a scavenger because he is always browsing along the bottom looking for any stray bits of food which the others might have left.

Spawning has been a mystery until lately, when it was found that these fish build a sort of bubble-nest (described in the glossary on page 156) at the surface of the water.

If you consider yourself expert in netting fishes, try catching one of these in a well-planted aquarium some time.

Symphysodon discus

Since his introduction in 1933, the *Symphysodon discus* from the Amazon has supplanted the Angelfish as the "King of Aquarium Fishes." His unusual pancake shape, along with beautiful colors and regal bearing, make him unforgettable even if seen only once.

A financial bonanza awaits the breeder who can get these fish to spawn regularly. They have always been expensive, because their large size necessitates the use of big, heavy shipping containers. Because of their size, they also require plenty of room in an aquarium and a good supply of live foods.

Young fish are sometimes much cheaper in price. However, watch out, because these have proven to be a bit difficult to raise. They are finicky about their food, and are not at all unlikely to go on a hunger strike if things are not to their liking. Although they might eventually accept food when they get hungry enough, their weakened condition at this time then makes them a prey to any ailment that comes along.

Botia macracantha

Because the brilliantly contrasting colors of this beauty look painted on, we have come to know this fish as the Clown Loach. They have not been bred in captivity, to the best of our knowledge, so we must depend upon high-priced imported stock from the East Indies. These fish seem to take well to a life in captivity, and live for quite a good life span. One thing we do know is that they are nocturnal in habits, and in a brightly-lighted aquarium they are distinctly ill at ease and will make every effort to hide beneath a rock or plant leaf, to become active again when the light is dim.

As with so many other attractive aquarium fishes, we have here another species which may some day be bred by the thousands, when some clever aquarist finds out how to do it.

Puntius titteya

(Above) The first of this group is the Cherry Barb, a small Barb, seldom exceeding 2½ inches. The female is tan-colored with chocolate-brown stripes, and the male becomes suffused with a glowing cherry-red at spawning time. A beautiful, peaceful fish.

Helostoma temmincki

(Below) This is the wild (but rare) variety of Kissing Gourami (fully described on page 73), which often has a yellow-brown or yellow-green color.

Xiphophorus helleri

It is rare that the albino form of any animal is more beautiful than the original wild form. But one exception to the rule is this Albino Sword-tail. This fish first appeared in aquarists' tanks over 30 years ago and there have been so many different albino varieties since then that they appear in four or five different colors. This one is the most attractive of the lot! (Regular color variety of this fish is shown on page 26.)

There is another interesting feature about this particular strain of albino. Ordinary albino Swordtails when crossed with wild Swordtails will only have wild colored offspring; this strain when crossed with Wild Swordtails will have Golden Swordtail babies, the only difference being in the color of the eyes. All true albino fishes have red eyes (the red comes from the blood vessels showing through); the Golden Swordtail has black eyes.

Aphyosemion cognatum

Africa has been very kind to aquarists by giving us many beautiful fishes, such as the one pictured above. This is one of the newer importations, and it is very likely that the name may be changed.

By any name it is a lovely fish, and it is sincerely hoped that American aquarists will soon breed this Panchax beauty in numbers. For some mysterious reason, it seems that the commercial breeders steer clear of the *Aphyosemion* species. The strange thing is that, while not extremely prolific, the fish is quite easy to breed, as are most of the others of this genus.

Have you noticed something odd about this fish? The shape of its dorsal fin makes it look as if Mother Nature were playing tricks and had it glued on backwards.

Puntius tetrazonus (Albino variety)

Recently we received a telephone call from Hugo Walter, a well-known breeder, who told us that he had raised a number of albino Tiger Barbs and was breeding them. He brought us a color picture of this attractive novelty, which we are happy to reproduce here. Compare this picture with that of a normal colored pair on page 45. Note how the normally black bands are white on the albino specimens, and the lighter portions on the normal ones are actually a deeper shade of pink on Mr. Walter's fish! This pink shade is so pronounced that we put them in the "Reds" section, rather than the "Vertical Stripes and Markings" section, where the normal colored ones belong.

We predict a bright future for this beautiful fish.

Capoeta hulstaerti

This is one of the most exciting African importations in recent years. The picture shows two pairs; the males are easily recognizable by their gold and black dorsal fins, which are colorless in the females, as well as the anal fins. At first the only ones which came in were males. As sometimes happens, the collectors may have discarded the less brilliantly colored specimens, thinking they were another species.

The Germans were quick to dub them "Schmetterlingsbarbe" (Butterfly Barbs), which seems to be an apt name for them. Spawnings have only resulted in mediocre success, and it may be quite a while before we see them in any numbers.

Corydoras melanistius brevirostris

Every time a *Corydoras* species is brought up from South America, the ichthyologists have more reason to scratch their heads. For instance, this particular group of *Corydoras melanistius* already has three sub-species: *C. melanistius melanistius, C. melanistius longirostris,* and the sub-species which is pictured here, *C. melanistius brevirostris.*

All three have the marking on the shoulder which extends up into the dorsal fin, and the band on the head which extends through the eye. The difference is that the *C. melanistius melanistius* has smaller spots, the *C. melanistius longirostris* has a longer snout, and our friend here has a shorter snout. All three are attractive, and also useful in that they keep the aquarium well cleared of excess food.

They are fairly active, but not so active in their rooting and poking around that they stir up a great deal of debris or uproot plants. Breeding them is far from an impossibility, but is not so simple that a beginner can do it.

Puntius filamentosum

This Barb is so new that an encyclopedia published in 1954 does not include him. We venture to predict that this fish will take his place right along with the most popular members of this family.

He is not large (the picture shows them at about life-size), and his coloring speaks rather plainly for itself. At times, the black tips at the ends of the tail lobes are more pronounced.

As with many other fishes, in the bare tanks of a dealer, you may not even recognize these fish. They make themselves as inconspicuous as possible, because of the lack of hiding places. This is their natural, instinctive reaction. The black tips on the tail fin disappear, the bright red in the fins are just barely pink, and even the pronounced black spot becomes much lighter than the picture shows.

Barbs are usually easy to breed. These should present no great difficulty, as they breed like ordinary Goldfish.

Corynopoma riisei

This fish, the Swordtail Characin, is so distinctive that he can't be confused with any other fish.

First note the four or five greatly elongated fin-rays in the lower tip of his sword-like tail. His real mark of distinction, however, is a long, paddle-like extension of his gill-plates. (Both of these features are confined to the male.) These paddles are usually held close to the body, but are extended while spawning. They are believed to be intromittent organs for conveying the sperm into the female's body, in a similar manner to the gonopodium (see glossary) of the live-bearing species.

This theory is borne out by accounts where females have deposited fertile eggs when there was no male fish in the tank to fertilize them in the usual manner. There is still some uncertainty and guessing with this fish although he has been well-known for a long time.

Puntius conchonius

The Rosy Barb is probably the most popular of the medium-sized Barbs, and deservedly so. Unfortunately the blush which gives them their name is not always present, but when conditions are to their liking it is usually more or less in evidence, and it becomes a deep red when spawning is going on. They are easy to keep, and seldom give any trouble to their tankmates.

Spawning them presents no difficulties, and they are very prolific; in fact, we have heard of people breeding them until they did not know what to do with them all. Commercial breeders raise huge numbers of them in pools.

This is a good fish for a hobbyist who wants to breed one of the Barb species, and has had no previous experience.

Betta splendens (Albino variety)

Here we see a pale, ghost-like albino of the Siamese Fighting Fish, *Betta splendens*. (The colored varieties are pictured on page 109.) He has rose-colored flesh, sometimes so transparent that his internal organs are visible. He has red, bloodshot eyes and is almost blind. Temperament and plenty of color (in the other varieties), combined with a unique elegance of movement, place this little scrapper in a class by himself.

The male Fighting Fish will attack any other male of the same species and will usually fight until one gives up. They feed on insects and small water animals but will also harm other smaller fish, and will eat the young new-born babes of the live-bearers.

In Thailand, where these fish have been domesticated for many years, the breeders stage fights between their fish, and place bets on the result.

In breeding, these fish first build a bubble-nest near the surface, and as soon as this is built, the male and female should be left alone in the thickly-planted tank. The male then approaches the female, spreading out his beautiful fins, and gradually maneuvers her toward the nest. If she is slow in responding, he may attack her fiercely. If she acquiesces, however, she is guided below the nest where the male wraps his body around hers and they perform a complicated rolling motion in the water.

She drops eggs during this movement, and the male fertilizes them at once. He then picks them up in his mouth and encloses each in a bubble of air, so that they rise to the bubble-nest on the surface. The act may be repeated until as many as 500 eggs are in the nest. Once this is complete, the male takes charge of the nest and chases the mother away. Now it is a good idea to remove the female before the male attacks her and, perhaps, even kills her.

Anoptichthys jordani

Here is an example of how a fish might lose its pigmentation, without being an albino. These interesting fish were found in a cave in Mexico, where there was absolutely no light. They were originally washed into this cave and stranded there. As there was no need for pigmentation in the total darkness, they lost their silvery colors and stopped developing pigmentation in their cells.

They were provided with normal eyes originally. However, after generations of disuse, the eyes gradually atrophied and then disappeared altogether. As with the blind, other senses of the fish became more acute. They were able to locate food and each other by a sense of taste, sound and smell, and lived a normal existence.

One strange sense which these blind fish have developed is a sort of "radar." They never bump into things, always turning away as they sense their closeness. Bats do this by emitting high-pitched screeches and listening to the echo. How does the Blind Cave Fish do it?

Etroplus maculatus

The Orange Chromide, as the *Etroplus maculatus* is popularly called, and the recently introduced *Etroplus suratensis* are the only members of the extensive Cichlid family to come to us from the East Indies.

In bodily appearance the Orange Chromide resembles our North American Sunfishes. His disposition is somewhat similar, too. When small he may be kept in a community aquarium with a fair amount of safety. When he grows up, though, he is liable to adopt a "chip on the shoulder" attitude, and must then be kept only with fishes able to take care of themselves in an argument.

If the Orange Chromide were a bit less attractive (like the *E. suratensis*), he might suffer a similar fate and drop off into obscurity. His lovely colors make him worthy of being kept, however. The background color is orange, and the male is peppered with red dots. At breeding time, the under part of the body takes on a dusky hue.

These fish breed easily.

Xiphophorus maculatus (Gold Wag variety)

Here is a fish which was developed with the medical profession in mind. The black pigment cells have given researchers in cancer much valuable information for their work.

The hobby has also gained a new strain of black-finned live-bearing fishes which are a joy to behold in any aquarium. The black fins have also been bred to the ever-popular Swordtail in all of the color varieties.

This is just one more of the seemingly endless possibilities to be produced by interbreeding the various species and strains of the *Xiphophorus* genus; every time we think we've seen them all, along come some more!

Tetraodon species

Salt water fishermen may be acquainted with the little nuisance known as the Blowfish, who chews their bait and gets on their hooks when they are trying for something bigger. The salt-water Blowfish are common in most parts of the world, and a few species are native to fresh waters in the Malay Peninsula.

The fresh-water species pictured here is a recent importation which we believe to be of the genus *Tetraodon,* but he has not yet been assigned a specific name. Looked at from above, a large figure "8" appears on his back, which gives him the popular name of "Figure 8 Puffer."

These fish are very comical aquarium inhabitants, with their eternal inquisitiveness and waddling swimming motions. Their means of protection, when frightened, is to blow themselves up like tiny balloons, making themselves look bigger. At the same time, they push out hundreds of tiny spines, making themselves highly unpalatable to bigger fishes.

Pachypanchax playfairii

Not many fishes come to us from East Africa, Tanzania and the Seychelles Islands, where this colorful fish is found. We have here a fish with a peculiarity which makes positive identification really easy. He can be recognized by touch alone—his scales stand out slightly, as on a fish with dropsy. Yet, as can be seen by the picture, he is a pretty fish.

Occasional individuals of this species get a bit rough with their companions. Sometimes a fish of this nature can be tamed by putting him in with fish a little rougher than he is.

This species is also very rugged under abuse. The thermostat on a certain dealer's tank got stuck at night and the temperature rose to over 100 degrees before the calamity was discovered. All the fishes, even including snails, were found dead, except for a dozen *P. playfairii* who were still living and suffered no ill effects!

Xiphophorus variatus

This is the well-known "Platy Variatus." Some fish of this species have a yellow dorsal fin and tail, some have a yellow dorsal and red tail, some have both dorsal and tail red, some have two black spots at the tail base, some have a crescent-shaped mark at the tail base, some have a black stripe at the top and bottom of the tail, and others have countless other patterns. That is the reason this fish has been given the specific name *variatus,* meaning "variegated."

The unfortunate female has little color, besides a muddy brown. Many interesting variations have been developed by selective breeding, and the fish may also be used for hybridization with other *Xiphophorus* species.

A little patience is required when raising the young; the males do not show their colors until they approach maturity. The pair shown here is about life size. The female is pictured above the male.

Xiphophorus helleri (Red variety)

Selective breeding can get wonderful results, especially when combined with hybridization. This fish, the Red Swordtail, is an outstanding example of the fish-breeder's art.

The first step in the production of this fish was to evolve an all red Platy. This was accomplished by breeding from wild stock which showed red blotches, and carefully inbreeding the ones with the most red until after many generations the Red Platy was produced.

Then there was the problem of transmitting this red to the Swordtail. Crossing the two resulted in a hybrid which had a short sword and some of the red color. Then came more close inbreeding to get rid of the Platy characteristics and bring out the Swordtail characteristics, the longer body and long sword, plus the red color. Amazingly enough, this has been done.

Polycentrus schomburgki

We rarely see this member of the Nandid family. Natives of Trinidad and Guiana, they are very fond of large pieces of living foods, such as cut-up garden worms or young fish. If you are not prepared to feed live foods, do not figure on keeping *P. schomburgki*.

These interesting fish can be kept in a community aquarium, but first take notice of their huge mouth; they can swallow a full-grown male Guppy with ease, so keep them with bigger fishes. One thing can be said for them: "If they can't swallow it, they won't bother it."

The male, of course, is the larger fish with the light dots. Don't count on seeing the dots all the time, though; they can disappear in a matter of moments, and the fish can become light or dark, according to his mood.

Carnegiella strigata

Relative of the *Carnegiella marthae* (page 147) is the *C. strigata*, the Marble Hatchet Fish. The colors in the picture give you a good idea of the beautiful iridescent quality of the fish's coloring. In order to get the proper view of this iridescence, your light must be properly placed, not behind the fish, not above the fish, but in front of the fish.

If your aquarium is opposite a window, and the viewer has the light coming from behind him and shining on the fish, then he will see this fish under the optimum of lighting conditions.

This is the beauty among the Hatchet Fishes, but also one of the most delicate ones. Perhaps where he comes from he feeds upon certain foods, for instance, live flies, which we cannot duplicate. He is certainly adapted by Nature for leaping up out of the water and catching flies.

This lovely fish has spawned on a few rare occasions.

Serrasalmus brandti

What is the most feared fish in the world? Some may name the shark, or perhaps the Barracuda. However, in Brazil and among people who know the Piranha, he gets the vote. No Brazilian native will go swimming in waters where he knows these man-eating Piranhas are.

Some of the tales one hears about these horrible fish may seem to be made up, but we once saw a particularly convincing demonstration in a scene from a motion picture. A large ham was dangled overboard from a small boat. It was immediately surrounded by a ravenous horde of Piranha fish, and in about 30 seconds there was nothing left but a bone.

If you dare to buy one, you should realize that they must be fed living fishes. They have hard heads and if your tank is so large that they can gain momentum, they will crash right through the glass.

Ctenopoma congicum

Brown and yellow are the main colors of this attractive fish, which comes to us from the Congo region in Africa. This is the only popular Anabantid from this region; his nearest relative is the famous Climbing Perch, the *Anabas testudineus,* which is native to the East Indies, quite a distance away.

We have not heard of this fish being imported in large quantities into the United States as yet. He is found in shallow waters which are well overgrown with plant life, and the female is said to build a bubble-nest somewhat similar to the Dwarf Gourami, *Colisa lalia.* The young are reputed to be very easy to raise.

This may well become one of our popular fishes of this type, and may supplant some of the Gouramies in the hearts of the fanciers. He is peaceful, and does not become too big for the average aquarist: about 3 inches is the size given.

Mollienisia latipinna (Albino variety)

Here we have an albino, the popular Sailfin Mollie. It is interesting to note that there is not a complete absence of color cells, but the black pigmentation has been toned down greatly. Where there is a bright blue in the normal fish, the albino shows a light green. By the same token, red markings become a light, attractive pink; and where the body is just silvery, it becomes a creamy yellow.

Mollies are very common in Florida, where they are sometimes used for bait. We have seen examples not only of albinism, but also of xanthism (see glossary) in the Golden Mollie, and melanism in the famous Black Mollie (page 106). Albinos are seldom found in the wild state, and black specimens almost never. A fish which stands out becomes a target for attackers, and does not live to a ripe old age.

Helostoma temmincki

This is the golden form of the popular Kissing Gourami. The photographer had an *Aplocheilus lineatus* barge into the picture just when the Gouramies went into their kissing act, and he got a bit more than he had bargained for. "Kissing" seems to be more popular among the younger Gourami specimens. This news probably comes as a shock to nobody.

The "kiss" is a comical thing to watch, but usually when you want them to show off, they just won't do it!

Gouramies' kissing is probably not an act of love but a mysterious compulsion that starts when the fish are 10 weeks old. Kissing is not confined to couples of opposite sexes.

Their thick, rubbery lips are not just used for kissing each other, either. These fish are generously provided with small teeth, and an appetite for green food is satisfied by "kissing" plants, glass, and rocks. So popular has this golden form of Gourami become that it is now virtually impossible to get specimens of the original green type (see page 51) any more, while the golden ones can be purchased almost anywhere.

Hyphessobrycon "robertsi"

We await a real name for this beautiful fish, which arrived recently from South America. The aquarium world has been fortunate lately in receiving a number of new and unidentified Tetra species like this one. The lower fish is obviously the male, with his better developed dorsal and anal fins and brighter colors.

Perhaps the generic name *Hyphessobrycon* is also an assumption which may turn out to be incorrect, but you will agree that it certainly *looks like* one of the *Hyphessobrycon* group. The only positive way we can be sure is to turn over some preserved specimens to a trained taxonomist, who takes from them such information as scale counts, fin-ray counts, head and body measurements, and an examination of the bone structure. This information is compared with other known measurements, and only then do we know if we have something new, and to what family it belongs.

Hyphessobrycon flammeus

The Red Tetra, sometimes called the Flame Tetra or Tetra from Rio, is one of the hardy perennials of the international fish world. This picture overstates his size by about one-fourth.

The male (on the right) has the brilliant red anal fin edged with black. His pelvic fins, which look black in the picture, are actually deep red with black tips. The entire latter half of the body is suffused with red. This coloring is also shared by the females, who are only a shade less handsome than their mates.

The Red Tetra is a fish with no bad habits: he doesn't nip fins, he doesn't chase other fishes, he eats anything, he is not a bit delicate, and breeds very easily. What more could anyone ask?

As the name indicates, these fish are native to waters around Rio de Janeiro. They have been with us a long time, having first been imported in 1920.

Belontia signata

This fish is sometimes referred to as the "Comb Tail." When the tail is spread, a fringe can be seen on both male and female. This is not shown very clearly in the picture, as both tails were folded when it was taken.

As may be assumed by his longer fins and deeper colors, the male is on the left. The female spawns by releasing a mass of eggs which float at the surface among the floating plants.

These fish resemble the Paradise Fish (page 43) a great deal; the difference is that they require warmer temperatures, coming as they do from Ceylon and Java. Eighty degrees is about right for your tank.

The young are large at hatching time, grow rapidly, and may well attain a length of five inches. As they are not very often imported or bred, you might have to do a bit of searching before you find this one at a dealer's.

Ctenops pumilis

These little beauties are not seen very often in the United States. They should become very popular, because they have everything in their favor. That they are beautiful is readily seen. Unlike their relatives, the Siamese Fighting Fish, or *Betta splendens* (page 60), they are peaceful; so peaceful, in fact, that the parents do not even have to be removed from the young after they become free-swimming.

There is another member of the genus, the *Ctenops vittatus* or Croaking Gourami, which does not have the striking colors of his cousin here, but is able to emit a croaking or purring noise. The *C. pumilis* comes from Thailand and the Malay Peninsula, and the *C. vittatus* from Burma.

Hyphessobrycon callistus

There seems to be much confusion about the name of this fish. There are three fish at least who have been called *H. callistus* at some time or other, and some hobbyist might even take issue with us on the naming of this one.

This fish reminds us a great deal of the Flame Tetra (page 75). Both fish are usually in good supply, and both are well worth having.

If the fancier has room for only one aquarium and that must be a small one, a collection of the smaller members of the *Hyphessobrycon* family is both colorful and interesting. They are all small, highly colored and peaceful.

Aphyocharax rubropinnis

Got a glass cover on your aquarium? If not, get one before you put in some of these Bloodfins. They are active and fond of jumping out of the water.

This fish has been one of the hardy perennials of the fish world, and is still enjoying a great deal of popularity today. His body is a light, gleaming blue and his fins are blood-red, as the name denotes.

The male (on the left) has a characteristic which only a few other fishes possess; his anal fin has an invisible hook on it, so if you net a Bloodfin and he hangs upside down from your net when you place him into the tank, that's the male!

This peaceful fish comes to us from the La Plata basin in South America.

Hyphessobrycon pulchripinnis

This is the Lemon Tetra, not a brightly colored fish, but nevertheless a fish with a charm all its own.

Native to the Amazon basin, he may look like nothing at all in a bare tank, as we would see him at most dealers', but he turns into something pretty as soon as he gets into the proper surroundings.

His body is a light lemon yellow, making a nice contrast with some of the other Tetras in which red or black predominates. He is one of the most peaceful of all the Tetras. As for size, the pair in the picture is either slightly enlarged or a very large pair.

Breeding is accomplished in a similar manner to all Characins (see glossary). The fry are easily raised once they have gone through the early stages of growth.

Carassius auratus

There may be some argument that this fish, the Goldfish, should not appear in a book of "tropical" aquarium fishes. Nonetheless, the fancy varieties of Goldfish today are the result of much intensive selective breeding over many generations, and they do much better when provided with a bit of heat.

To be exact, some of the so-called "tropical" fishes have been known to withstand quite a lot of cold. There have been cases, for instance, of Paradise Fish surviving almost freezing temperatures.

The Chinese were the first to breed the Goldfish, the most popular of all aquarium fishes, hundreds of years ago. Later the Japanese also took up the art, and now many of the finest strains come from Japan. There are many strains from both countries, some of which have very long fins, some bulging eyes, some knobbly scales, and others known for their round heads.

Xiphophorus Hybrid (Red Jets)

The Red Jet Swordtail was developed by the famous geneticist Dr. Myron Gordon, by crossing a hybrid between *Xiphophorus helleri* and *Xiphophorus montezumae* with a normal *Xiphophorus helleri*. Strange that there is so much black in the tail fin, and the dorsal fins of both male and female are almost clear!

As sometimes happens when a deep black color is developed, the parts which are pigmented a deep black are very apt to become cancerous, resulting in a dead or deformed fish, whose tail fin rots away.

Hyphessobrycon heterorhabdus

For many years, we have been seeing a very pretty Tetra which the dealers have been calling *Hemigrammus ulreyi*. Although it has been positively identified as *Hyphessobrycon heterorhabdus,* the old name still stubbornly hangs on. Finally we have gotten a *real Hemigrammus ulreyi*, and are able to show it to you below.

Pyrrhulina species

We have a new *Pyrrhulina* here, but none of the descriptions of the different species seem to apply to this one. He is one of a new species that have not been bred to date, or if they have, the facts have not been published.

Whatever the case may be, we have a beautiful as well as peaceful fish here. The only one of this genus we know is the *P. rachoviana,* and they place their eggs on a broad leaf of a plant, or in the absence of this, on a rock or the bottom slate of the aquarium. Here the eggs are fanned and guarded by the male. They hatch in two days, after which time the parents should be removed from the tank.

Puntius gelius

One of our smallest Barbs is this fellow who comes from India, and is included in only a few collections. This reticence on the part of aquarists is probably because the colors of this fish are not quite as resplendent as those of some of his cousins. He is a model citizen of the community aquarium in every other way. In size he is a bit smaller than the picture, and his body is somewhat longer and slimmer than the rest of the family, making him look like a member of the *Rasbora* genus.

These fish spawn readily in the usual Barb fashion. After a lively chase the male drives the female into a plant thicket. Here she stops, evidently realizing what is expected of her. He comes alongside, and they press their bodies together, quivering, until a few eggs are expelled and sprayed by the male. They drop into the plants and stick there.

If left in the aquarium after spawning, these fish are very quick to eat all the eggs, so net them out as soon as you see them hunting.

Brachygobius xanthozonus

Ever notice the short body and alternating black and yellow colors of a bumblebee? Nothing in the fish world could remind you more of a bumblebee than the *B. xanthozonus*.

This pretty and interesting fish comes to us from the rice paddies and jungle streams of Malaya. This is not the most active of fish. Sexes are difficult to distinguish, but it is usually possible to recognize a female by her greater girth and slightly paler color in the last yellow band. These fish are able to adhere to solid objects by their ventral fins, which are united and form a suction disc.

Spawnings are infrequent and often unsuccessful. The female attaches her eggs to the underside of a rock or the inside of a flowerpot. The male then evicts his mate and takes charge, guarding the eggs until they hatch.

Haplochromis wingati

The editors have a personal interest in this beautiful Mouthbreeder. Three young specimens about half the size of the female (lower fish) arrived in an African shipment, and they looked to us like one of the many *Tilapia* species, most of which get to be large, unattractive and rough. Curiosity got the better of us, however, and when they grew up, we were rewarded with the beauties above. They were identified as *Haplochromis wingati,* and did not exceed the size shown here.

They are easily bred; the female carries 40 to 60 eggs in her mouth for two weeks until they hatch, and then shelters the young in her mouth until they get too big to fit in.

Unfortunately, these fish will chew up tender plants, and some vegetable matter should be provided in their diet.

Puntius stoliczkai

This Barb looks like a happy combination. He has the nice red and black dorsal of the *Puntius ticto,* and the rosy belly of the *Puntius conchonius.* He may be distinguished by the fact that where the *P. ticto* is of a green hue, he is a silver blue.

Like the other large Barbs, this fish should not be kept with thread-finned fish like the Angelfish or Gouramies. They might behave themselves, but there is always the great possibility that fins will be mistaken for worms.

This beauty comes to us from India, and is not seen often in the tanks of American aquarists. If someone were to spawn these fish, another "standby" might be established.

Cichlasoma festivum (on right page, bottom)

Cichlasoma festivum is known as the "Flag Cichlid" and comes from the same parts of the Amazon as the Angelfish. His diagonal line distinguishes him from all other aquarium fishes.

Hypostomus plecostomus

(Above) A friend, on first seeing this fish, suggested a slight name change—to "Preposterous." Some fish are odd, but he goes one step further; *he's ugly!* Therein lies his greatest charm; he's such a comic caricature that he's bound to attract attention. He's useful too: he keeps plants and glass tank sides clear of algae.

Corydoras agassízi

The *Corydoras* has inherited the job once done by the snails, and he does it much better. It was once the custom to put a few snails into an aquarium, on the theory that they would clean it up. Their usefulness was limited, however, and their prolific habits soon resulted in many snails. This in turn resulted in chewed plants, and a great quantity of droppings, which they were supposed to clean up in the first place. They were also practically impossible to eradicate without cleaning out the aquarium and discarding the plants. The *Corydoras* has none of these bad habits and, besides, is much more attractive than a snail, notwithstanding the fact that he is no beauty.

Corydoras microps

The *Corydoras* family is frequently described as "attractive" and "useful," but it does not usually provide us with a species which can also be described as "beautiful," which may well be applied to *Corydoras microps,* with their pattern of gleaming white spots on an inky black background.

It is not usually as easy to distinguish males, the upper fish in this picture, with most species of *Corydoras*. As a rule they are a little smaller, and the body of the female shows up much wider when viewed from above.

Most of us never tire of watching *Corydoras* poking around on the bottom, rolling their eyes and twitching their whiskers, eternally searching for (and finding) food which the others have missed. Their excited glee when they find a few tubifex worms is very comical to behold.

Cyprinodon nevadensis

Those who live along the Atlantic coast will immediately recognize the similarity between this fish and the common Pursy or Sheepshead Minnow, *Cyprinodon variegatus*. They are indeed members of the same genus. The Nevada desert lands were once a part of the ocean, as is proved by fossil deposits, and it seems these fish were able to make the gradual transition to fresh water when the ocean withdrew thousands of years ago and left them there.

Mollienisia latipinna   (on right page, bottom)

We have already seen the Albino Mollie on page 72. This picture gives us the true colors of the normal Sailfin Mollie.

Aphyosemion gardneri

For a long time this fish has been known, especially to beginning aquarists, as *Aphyosemion arnoldi*. For a while the yellow variation alone was called *Aphyosemion gardneri*; now both the yellow and reddish-blue fish are grouped under this name. Shakespeare's statement about a rose by any other name smelling as sweet certainly applies here.

The body is steel-blue, and the dots and markings are wine-red, with a stripe of yellow appearing in the anal fin and the lower part of the tail.

This handsome fish buries its eggs among plant roots at the bottom, and they may take as long as three or four weeks to hatch. The illustration shows them at about life size.

Apistogramma ramirezi

German aquarists have aptly named these "Schmetterlingsbunt-barschen," or "Butterfly Cichlids." Since their introduction in 1947, they have attained a huge popularity both in the United States and abroad. This popularity of course is well-deserved.

An unusual trait is the fact that the female is not the "ugly duckling" as with most Dwarf Cichlids. As can be seen in the picture, she (the fish in front) is a good match for his colors, even surpassing him at times. The males can be distinguished by their longer dorsal rays, which still have a little growing to do in this male.

This fish enjoys a slightly higher temperature than most, 80 to 82 degrees suiting him well. At this temperature they spawn readily, but are not at all unlikely to eat their own eggs or fry.

Megalamphodus megalopterus

Our good friend Harald Schultz in Brazil has known this fish for five years and thought it to be a new species of *Hyphessobrycon,* which it certainly resembles. We were finally able to obtain some and get them identified. We have the honor of introducing the aquarium hobby to the first *Megalamphodus* species to be seen so far. The Black Phantom Tetra is found in the region of the Guaporé River in Brazil, and the pair shown here is slightly larger than life size. Males (upper fish) have higher dorsal fins and deeper anal fins, which are jet black when the fish is not frightened. As can be seen here, the females have smaller fins, and the ventrals are red.

We hope this fish turns out to be a ready breeder; it will definitely become another favorite among aquarists in the future.

Labeo bicolor

For fully a year before aquarists determined the scientific name of this fish, he was known solely as the Red-Tailed Black Shark. As you can see, he has only two colors, the deep black of the body, and the bright red of the tail. He is closely related to the *Botia macracantha* (page 50).

Native to Thailand and Indonesia, this is one of the larger aquarium fishes; he may attain a length of as much as 10 inches.

Nothing is known about the breeding habits of this beautiful fish. A financial bonanza probably awaits the first aquarist to accomplish the feat of breeding the species.

Besides being a peaceful fish, the Black Shark is also an excellent scavenger for your tank.

Gasteropelecus levis

Note the extra long pectoral fins which resemble the wings of an insect. It is said that these fish actually make a buzzing noise when they leap from the water. This may be caused by the fins in beating the air, but this has not been definitely ascertained.

The difficulty in keeping these fish is due to the fact that they are not easy to feed. Any food which sinks below the surface for any distance is not pursued and is lost to them when the other fish get it away.

This fish is native to the vicinity of Para in Brazil.

Cichlasoma meeki

This is one of the most popular of the larger Cichlids. He comes to us from Yucatan and is named after Professor Seth Meek who introduced him in 1918. He was first brought into the United States in 1936 where he made an immediate hit.

The colors of this fish are without doubt the reason for his great popularity. At spawning time, the belly of the male becomes a fiery red. This red reaches all the way up past the gill covers and even into the mouth. For this reason, fanciers have named him the Fire-mouth Cichlid.

So peaceful is this fish that he has been known to raise a family in a community tank, a feat which probably calls for the utmost in diplomacy in the fish world. This fish spawns like other Cichlids and the young are very easily raised.

Cichlasoma biocellatum

Look at the heavy chin and aggressive mouth of this fish. Do you wonder that he has been called "Jack Dempsey"? This is one of the really large Cichlids and if it were not for his very attractive colors he would probably be highly unpopular for his bad temper.

This is a fish to be kept in company only with its own kind or with other large fishes who are well able to take care of themselves.

In color this fellow is a smoky black with bright blue spots becoming yellow towards the tail. Against this background, the fiery red eye stands out like a jewel.

A well-mated pair usually prove to be devoted parents and are very likely to produce many offspring.

Chanda ranga

It is hard to believe that these beautiful little fish are so numerous in their native India that they are often used for fertilizer. This is especially startling when we realize the difficulty so often encountered when attempts are made to spawn them in captivity.

Their great transparency of body is the reason they are popularly known as Glass Fish. Actually they have some color, a light amber set off by black tips on the dorsal fin. The male has the additional ornament of a bright blue edge on the second dorsal and anal fins, which the female largely lacks.

Although these fish spawn readily, the fry are so tiny that it is only with extreme difficulty that any number of them can be raised. Eggs are laid in plant thickets and the parents should be removed after spawning is completed.

Aplocheilus panchax

For many years this fish, from India, Burma, Thailand and the Malay Archipelago, was known to aquarists as *Panchax panchax,* and the name still persists.

Colors of this fish may vary anywhere from light tan to dark olive. Blue-green dots adorn the sides of the male, the upper fish in this picture.

This species is highly recommended to beginners who wish to try their luck in this particular family. These fish spawn among the plants at the top and the eggs may be seen hanging there. The usual procedure is to remove them and place them in a smaller container where they hatch in about two weeks. The young become free-swimming almost at once, and grow rapidly thereafter if properly fed.

Distichodus affinis

The Stanley Pool region of the Belgian Congo is very rich in fish life, as-has been proven by Pierre Brichard, who has been responsible for many interesting introductions in the aquaria of hobbyists all over the world. This fish, although long known to science, was practically unknown to aquarists until he began shipping them. The red in the dorsal, anal and ventral fins is just about the most brilliant red we have ever seen in any fish; contrasted to the silvery body with its big eyes, our fish here is a real beauty.

There are a few drawbacks to its beauty, however: in the first place, they get quite large, and require a big aquarium. Another drawback is that they have an insatiable appetite for plants.

Chilodus punctatus

Most of our aquarium fishes swim horizontally. A few, like the Pencil-fishes, swim with their heads high and their tails down. Still others, like this one, swim with their heads bowed, but certainly not in shame.

The Spotted Headstander has everything to recommend it as an aquarium fish: it is peaceful, eats anything in the food line, and while it likes to browse along the bottom, will not uproot plants, nor will it nibble them. Do not be greatly disappointed if you do not get fish with such highly colored fins as these; they were collected in the Rio Guaporé by Harald Schultz and sent to us. The other variety with only a hint of pink in the fins is attractive as well, and they will surely become one of your favorites, if you do not already have them. Unfortunately, we have not as yet heard of a successful spawning.

Nannacara anomala

This Dwarf Cichlid comes from Guyana. The male (the upper fish in the illustration) has fins which are larger and more pointed than the much smaller female. He is also about half again as large in overall size. He is master in the home, a situation which is quickly reversed after spawning is completed. It is then a very comical sight to watch the little female go after the huge male and flip her tail in his face, spread her gill-covers, poke him and even nip him if he displays the least curiosity as to what is going on with the eggs.

There is another *Nannacara*, the *N. taenia*, who is about the same size. His sides have stripes, however, and sometimes there are vertical bars which give a latticed effect. This is especially noticeable in the female at spawning time.

Both species thrive very well in quite small aquaria.

Apistogramma ortmanni

This is one of the lesser known *Apistogramma* species. He does not have the flashy colors which distinguish some of his cousins but is nevertheless a very attractive little fish.

His habitat is the upper Amazon river.

The greatest attraction these fish have is that they may be kept and spawned in rather small aquaria. For instance, they can easily be propagated in a three-gallon aquarium.

Similar to other Dwarf Cichlids, this species has a very interesting family life. They especially seem to lend themselves to parenthood, and are probably the easiest of the Dwarf Cichlids to breed. At breeding time, the female actually outshines her much larger mate in color, developing a bright yellow body with an intense black stripe through the middle, and bright yellow fins.

Mollienisia latipinna

The picture shows male specimens of *Mollienisia latipinna* which are common along the coastal waters of Florida. The black one is our prized Black Mollie, which has been bred extensively by commercial breeders in Florida as well as by aquarists the world over. The black ones occur occasionally in nature, but seldom survive for long because their color makes them a target for other predatory fishes. Careful selective breeding has given us Black Mollies which breed almost 100 per cent true, but the comparatively close confines of an aquarium do not give them the same conditions that they would get in nature. Tank-raised Mollies are therefore inclined to be a bit smaller than their forebears and not quite as robust.

Pterophyllum eimekei (Black variety)

The Black Angelfish is at present supplanting the common variety in the hearts of fish hobbyists. The midnight black of its body, as well as its dignified bearing, is doing much to lend beauty to our aquaria. A black fish like this is especially lovely when placed with other fishes of a contrasting color, like a Red Swordtail or Red Platy. These colors against the green of the plants make an unforgettable combination.

Metynnis species

Although he bears a resemblance to the Piranha, to which he is related, the *Metynnis* is a comparatively mild specimen. He will seldom attack any but a much smaller fish.

He is quite showy, and his deep body has a very attractive appearance. He spends most of his time out in the open, a trait which is also in his favor.

One thing goes against him, however. He is very partial to vegetable food, which makes him a menace in a well-planted tank. Putting duckweed in his diet will help somewhat.

The only way completely to overcome his appetite for greenery is either to set up a tank which uses only rocks for decoration, or place a glass partition towards the rear of the tank and place your plants behind this, where the *Metynnis* can't get at them.

It will take a great deal of ingenuity to avoid the psychological drawback involved here: placing a fish under conditions of constant frustration. A national magazine once published a picture of a pig with a nervous breakdown; maybe a fish can be in the same fix.

Betta splendens (on right page, bottom) –

Here we have three examples of the different color varieties developed in the Siamese Fighting Fish (see description on page 60). All are males; the females have shorter fins, heavier bellies and less color.

Copeina arnoldi

This interesting fish is called the "Splashing Tetra" from the German aquarists' name for him, "Spritzsalmler." He and his mate have what is probably the most unusual method of spawning in all fishdom. Both fish jump out of the water and attach themselves to an overhanging leaf, where the female attaches the eggs and the male fertilizes them. Then they drop back into the water and take turns splashing water up to keep the eggs wet. When the fry hatch, they drop into the water.

Trichogaster leeri

This is the prince of all the Gouramies, the Pearl or Mosaic Gourami, who comes from Sumatra and Borneo. Since this fish's introduction to the United States his popularity has never waned.

The fish pictured here is a male, distinguished by his long dorsal fin and deep, fringed anal fin. His sides have a violet sheen in a proper light, and the dots which pepper the body and fins are pearly white. The black line which we see extending from the lips into the body is more distinct at times and extends to the caudal base. At spawning time, the male's throat and belly change from pure white to a deep orange.

Spawning is accomplished by the building of a bubble-nest, in the manner of most Labyrinth Fishes. (See next page.)

His quiet dignity and perfect manners make him an ideal fish for the community aquarium.

Trichogaster microlepis

Take a good look at a fish which is not too familiar to hobbyists of the United States. He will probably be known as the Silver Gourami. Even though there is an evident lack of striking colors in this fish, we predict that he will become popular.

The spawning habits of this family of fish are interesting to watch. The male frequently amuses himself by building bubble-nests, whether or not there is a female present. If there is a female and she is ready to spawn, he tries to get her under the nest when it is completed. When all is ready, she permits him to encircle her body and squeeze out a few eggs, which he immediately fertilizes. She sinks to the bottom exhausted while he picks up the eggs and pushes them into the bubble-nest. By the time he has finished this job she has recovered and the process is repeated until the eggs are all out. He then guards the nest until the fry have become free-swimming.

Pelmatochromis kribensis

Here we have the popular African (Congo) version of the Dwarf Cichlid (see next page).

The most striking feature of the male is the large, wine-red blotch on his sides. The female, which is the smaller and more drab of the two, really comes into her glory at breeding time. Her red blotch becomes deep in color, the forward half of her body bronze, and the back half a sooty-black.   (Below) This shows a young, not fully developed pair.

Pelmatochromis taeniatus

This fish was at first confused with *P. kribensis* (on the opposite page). The two are very similar, but it can be seen that the color pattern of the tail fin is different. We also get this species from the Congo, and their breeding habits are the same.

Small as they are, these fish should have at least an 8-gallon aquarium in which to spawn. Another rule to be strictly observed is never to put a pair together unless the female indicates by her bulging sides that she is ready to spawn. If the male is ready and the female is not, the situation could easily end with a dead female.

A deeply shaded spot should be provided. One of the best has been found to be a flowerpot with a notch broken out of the rim, covered with a flat piece of slate. The fish make themselves at home here, and will usually attach their eggs to the inside wall. These Cichlids have an unfortunate tendency to eat their own eggs or young.

Nannochromis nudiceps

When we first saw this fish it was known as *"Pelmatochromis taeniatus."* A look at page 113 will show how wide of the mark this name came.

This is one of the several beautiful Dwarf Cichlids to come from the Congo region of Africa. Previously a few occasional specimens came in, but today they are often available. This is not one of the easy ones to breed. As with the other Dwarf Cichlids, the best way to get a mated pair is to get a number of young ones and raise them together. Soon you will see pairs showing a preference for each other. Giving them their own quarters will often result in a spawning.

One thing this picture does not show is a wine-red blotch in the belly region, which is exceptionally in evidence when spawning is imminent.

Moenkhausia oligolepis

This fish has several attractive features: he has an exotic large, black spot at the base of his tail, and he has beautiful red eyes.

He also has some serious drawbacks, however. One is that he becomes quite large, attaining a length of 4 inches. This is sometimes a source of surprise to purchasers who are astonished to find how quickly their "cute little fish" becomes something bigger than they had bargained for.

Another trait *not* in his favor is his partly vegetarian appetite, which extends to the plants in an aquarium. In this regard, he is like the *Metynnis* species (page 108). This appetite can be partly satisfied by including duckweed in his diet, but he will still chew plants.

Phenacogrammus interruptus

(Above) This Tetra ranks as the most beautiful of all African Characins to reach the United States. They breed profusely in acid water in their native haunts and the young are easy to raise. They have been bred in captivity, but the feat is not supposed to be an easy one.

Trichogaster trichopterus

Whoever named this fish from India and the Malay Peninsula the "Three-spot Gourami" evidently had a lively imagination: there are only two spots on his body, one in the center and one at the base of his tail. (The eye was probably counted as the third spot.) There are two color varieties of this fish, the brownish striped fish, and the ones with the blue overcast, known as the *Sumatranus* variety. The latter has become so popular that we hardly ever see the other.

A peaceful fish, easy to keep, he is one of the easiest bubble-nest builders to spawn.

This is one of the few fishes who eat *Hydra* (voracious tiny clinging aquatic animals) when hungry. *Hydra* are often introduced inadvertently with live food, and are the very devil to eradicate once they have established themselves. They are also a real menace in a breeding tank, as they kill and eat fry.

– *Alestopetersius caudalus* (on left page, bottom)

This is a yellow counterpart of *Phenacogrammus interruptus,* and comes from the same region of Africa (Belgian Congo). His habits are the same and the two fish are often confused with each other.

Barilius christyi

For obvious reasons, this fish has often been known as the "Copper-nose." It is one of the very interesting species to come from the Belgian Congo, where the fish are often collected and shipped by Pierre Brichard.

This is a school fish, found in swarms at or near the surface. As the streamlined body indicates, this fish is an active swimmer and good jumper, and should be kept in a covered aquarium—a good idea with any fish.

The Coppernose will accept any food, but should not be fed anything which sinks to the bottom. In order to pick up anything, he must turn on his side. Do not keep him with smaller fishes, as he is very apt to torment them.

Synodontis decorus

This is another of the truly decorative Catfishes which come from Africa. Besides having big round spots on the sides, this one has smaller spots on his cheeks and dorsal fin and stripes on his tail.

Like many of the Catfishes, this species is largely nocturnal in habits, and is not often to be seen in the daytime or under artificial light. Care must be exercised when handling them; the strong first rays of the dorsal and pectoral fins lock into place when the fish is frightened, and their sharp points pierce the skin and flesh very easily. This is also a means of protection from being swallowed by larger fishes.

A peculiarity of this genus is that they can swim just as easily upside down as rightside up.

Lebistes reticulatus

This is the Guppy, undoubtedly the most popular and plentiful of all aquarium fishes. Selective inbreeding has led to the development of many beautiful strains. The color photograph illustrates the world famous Hahnel Guppies, who are noted for their intense coloration and long fins. Guppies are live-bearing fish and very prolific.

Lebistes reticulatus

The Guppies illustrated above are Sternke's fancy Guppies. They are noted for their fancy tails. Note the double swordtail effect. Below are some of the Hahnel strain.

Corydoras metae

This is one of the newest *Corydoras* species to come in, and a very attractive one it is. One of the difficulties of the family was encountered when spawning was attempted. Probably more would have been bred if they had been given their own quarters, but many aquarists keep them for a strictly utilitarian reason, one to a tank.

One of the first things we heard after the introduction of this fish is that *it spawned*. The female picks up the sperm directly from the male, at the same time releasing a few eggs which she carries in a pocket formed by her ventral fins. She swims up near the surface and pushes the sperm against the glass or a plant leaf, then pushes her belly against the spot where the sperm was placed and attaches the eggs there. Fry hatch in 5 days and are easily raised.

Hemigrammus unilineatus

"Feather Fin" is the name popularly applied to this species. The appearance of the black streak with the white border in the anal fin, and the black spot with the black tip in the dorsal fin, are the reasons for the name. A pink tail sets the fish off nicely.

Besides being attractive, this fish is also easily kept. He eats prepared foods as well as live with a great deal of enthusiasm. Like most other small Tetras, he enjoys swimming around in the open spaces, and is always there when you want to look at him.

Spawning them is a simple matter; they spawn in the regular Tetra fashion, and are apt to eat their eggs when finished.

Rivulus harti

(Above) This species, from Trinidad and Venezuela, differs from most of the other *Rivulus* species by the absence in the female of the well-known "Rivulus spot" (see glossary). This is one of the larger species, and attains a length of four inches.

Neolebias ansorgei

(Below) Another view, for comparison purposes, of the fish we have shown on page 5. The coloration of both sexes is similar. Look for the slenderer ones as a more or less accurate guide to the males.

Lebistes reticulatus

Without a doubt, the most popular aquarium fish is this one—the Guppy. (Also see pages 120, 121.)

This famous photograph is considered to be one of the best pictures of Guppies in existence. Taken by Mervin F. Roberts, it illustrates some of Hahnel's prize-winning stock.

Geophagus jurupari

The name *Geophagus* means "Earth-eater." This Cichlid is very fond of grubbing around on the bottom and sifting out bits of food from the gravel. This is not done so forcefully that the plants are uprooted, and the fish are peaceful as well as attractive, with their long snouts and big eyes.

Although this fish was once reputed to be a mouthbreeding species, it is now known to breed in the usual Cichlid manner, although the female sometimes shelters her young in her mouth when danger threatens.

The pair shown here are still young, and positive sexing is impossible. They have been known to attain a size of 6 inches in the aquarium.

Mimigoniates inequalis

Here is a fish which can "talk." It is capable of emitting tiny croaking sounds. These are made by gulping mouthfuls of air at the surface and forcing it out through the gills, which the fish does at times. This gives it two popular names, the Blue Tetra and the Croaking Tetra.

This is an active fish, which is often found in schools in the streams of southeastern Brazil. Because of its activity, plenty of swimming space is indicated, and of course a covered aquarium.

Although they have been spawned, the exact method of transmitting the sperm from the male to the female is not known. Females have been known to deposit fertile eggs after having been separated from the male.

Danio malabaricus

This Giant Danio is a well-known species from the Malabar coast and Ceylon. He is an active, colorful fish, who adds life to any aquarium. Breeding is easily accomplished; they spawn like Barbs, dropping adhesive eggs among fine-leaved plants.

Gnathonemus macrolepidotus

If African fishes had nightmares, they would probably see some of the forms which a perusal of a book on African fresh-water fish would show. This one has a knob on its lower jaw; others have blunt, turned-down snouts, some have beaks like birds, and still others have big bodies with ridiculously small heads. All are interesting, but most are too large for the average aquarium. Young specimens can be stunted somewhat when kept in smaller quarters, but it is very doubtful if the very interesting and freakish genera *Gnathonemus, Marcusenius, Mormyrus* and *Mormyrops* will ever be spawned in captivity. Some of these look like something from another world.

— *Rasbora argyrotaenia* (on left page, bottom)

If you were to see the name before seeing the fish, you would expect to see a fish with a silver stripe. The stripe is there, but its iridescence is such that the fish reflects a distinguishing violet sheen. The yellow, black-rimmed tail is also a thing of beauty.

Aequidens pulcher

This is the well-known Blue Acara, one of our popular Cichlids. One of the strongest reasons for its popularity is the fact that it breeds readily, and our picture shows a parent fish guarding eggs.

The family life of the Cichlids makes them exceptionally interesting to study. Parents guard their eggs and young, and once they have become free-swimming the little ones are continually herded by either one parent or the other, making a charming picture.

The Blue Acara should be kept with fishes of its own size, or better yet in an aquarium of its own.

Heríchthys cyanoguttatus

We are usually prone to think of Cichlids as coming from far-off tropical climes. Most rules have a few exceptions, and this fish is one of them. Known as the Texas Cichlid, *Herichthys cyanoguttatus* is native to the Rio Grande and other streams in southern Texas and has the distinction of being the only Cichlid native to this country. The dots which pepper the body become brilliant blue when the fish is about to spawn. Being one of the larger ones, roomy quarters are in order. If you intend to spawn this one, be prepared for a big family.

Hyphessobrycon (?) species

This fish may easily turn out to be a *Hemigrammus* or some other species of Characin. To the best of our knowledge, it has not as yet been classified. Were it not for the fact that Harald Schultz, a great ethnologist, is also deeply interested in aquatic biology, this fish might not have shown up for many a year.

The lower fish can be assumed to be the male, judging by its slimmer lines. They are very hardy, and absolutely peaceful even to smaller tank-mates. They eat everything, but do not touch the plants. If you are willing to forget about bright, flashy colors this little Tetra is a perfect aquarium fish.

Brachydanio kerri

Here is an additional member of the popular Danio group which is so well known to fish hobbyists all over the world. Whether it will be as well received as the other Danios have been is a question; the colors are not quite as interesting as in the other species, but it is just as active and hardy as the others.

The best way to get the most out of Danios in an aquarium is to keep them in a school of six or more. Here they show themselves in their best colors, and will chase around after each other all day. They lend a great deal of life to any aquarium.

Curimatus boulengeri

Here is one of the many species which seldom reach the aquaria of hobbyists. Although there is no riot of color, they make a good "contrast fish" and with proper lighting show a good deal of iridescence. They are excellent scavengers and do a lot of poking about the bottom of the tank.

The lower fish may be of a different species; all three were caught in the same pool in Brazil. It is also possible that the lack of the black spot in the caudal peduncle, as well as the slightly brighter colors, might mark the odd one as a male.

One thing we do know from our experience with *Curimatus argenteus*: they are perfectly peaceful and do not eat plants. This is more than we can say of some of our more colorful species.

Catoprion mento

Harald Schultz named this one the Wimple Piranha, because the high dorsal fin reminded him of the high peaked caps worn by the ladies in the Middle Ages. Although it is closely related to the true Piranhas (see page 70), it can be safely kept in a community aquarium because it does not have the dental equipment of its fearsome relations. The pugnacious jaw of the true Piranhas is there, lending it a warlike appearance which its behavior belies.

This fish has also made an appearance among German aquarists, and we have not yet had word of any spawnings. Seen head-on, the Wimple Piranha shows an extremely compressed body.

Arnoldichthys spilopterus

Here is a fish who is not easily mistaken, though closely related to the *Phenacogrammus interruptus* (page 116). He comes from West Africa, in the Niger basin. These fish travel in large schools in their native grounds and are very difficult to capture; they have a tricky habit of leaping over the net when it closes in on them.

The back is brownish, shading to metallic green on the sides, and the belly is silvery. The horizontal stripe is bordered on each side by a row of large scales, the dorsal fin has a large black spot, and the eyes are bright red. This is one of the fishes which becomes beautiful when lighted so that the iridescent sheen of his scales is reflected toward the observer.

We seldom see this beauty, for the reason that we still must depend on importations from Africa. This is one of many fishes awaiting the skill and patience of a talented aquarist to be bred.

Capoeta puckelli

Because it had two spots and was a Barb, dealers who first got this little fellow from Africa called it *"Puntius bimaculatus."* We sent preserved specimens for identification and soon got word that it was *Capoeta puckelli.*

As so often happens when a fish is photographed, this fish is not shown in its best colors. The dorsal and caudal fins are pink at the base, and there is a green horizontal stripe which promptly disappears when the fish is netted. Once they have become established in an aquarium which they find to their liking, it again puts in an appearance. This is one of the things which makes a fish photographer tear his hair out.

The lower fish is the male, and it may be added that ours have spawned readily, and are easily raised.

Moenkhausia dichroura

This pair of fish came in a shipment from South America, and we later had them identified. When we found out that they were a species of *Moenkhausia* it came as a complete surprise, because they did not resemble the *Moenkhausia oligolepis* (page 115) or *Moenkhausia pittieri*. Another thing which distinguished them was that they did not eat plants, like *Moenkhausia oligolepis*. They are peaceful, and it is hoped that more of them will make an appearance in this country.

The unusual color pattern of the tail is very similar to that of the Scissortailed Rasbora, *Rasbora trilineata*.

Puntius oligolepis

This is probably the most popular of the small Barbs. He is a native of the island of Sumatra, and was introduced to aquarists in 1925.

The male is easily distinguished by the black border on his dorsal and anal fins; his general coloring is brighter as well. The picture shows the fish at slightly less than full size. The sides are a reddish-brown, and there is an indistinct double horizontal line. The fins are orange in color. The scales are large in proportion to the size of the fish.

An excellent aquarium fish, he is contented with any food offered. He is useful also in that he will go over the bottom thoroughly, picking up any food which has dropped there and would otherwise foul.

In the manner of the other Barbs, they spawn readily.

Puntius holotaenia

This is one of the very rare Barbs that occasionally come from the Congo region in Africa. Young specimens of this fish are very attractively colored, with the fins a much brighter red than the picture shows. The large black spot on the dorsal fin is especially attractive. As the fish grows up, the colors seem to fade, a condition that changes when the fish are spawning.

Like most African Barbs, this species has not yet been spawned in captivity, but we suspect that the reason for this is more lack of availability than an unwillingness on the fish's part to cooperate.

Phallichthys amates

The "Merry Widow" is the name popularly applied to the live-bearer shown here. He comes from Honduras, and we do not see him as often as we once did.

The length of the male's gonopodium is the chief characteristic of this fish. This is the long, pointed fin with which the male live-bearer transmits his sperm into the body of the female, thereby making it possible for her to carry her young until they are born.

The reason why it is not possible to hybridize many species of live-bearing fishes is well illustrated here. This fish's extremely long gonopodium has a hook which points downward. Other fish have a shorter fin, some with a hook which points the other way. Others have a knob on the end. These mechanical differences may prevent the sperm from getting inserted, and in addition, there are biological differences which might not permit the cells to mingle.

Corydoras undulatus

This attractive *Corydoras* greatly resembles the *C. aeneus* (page 90) in body shape. The monotony of color is relieved in this fellow, however, by a great number of dark flecks in the upper portion of the body. He has been known to scientists since 1877, and was first introduced in 1938.

Here is a method of capturing these Catfish used by some collectors. They find a pool where the number of swirls on the surface tells them that there are good numbers of *Corydoras* present. They divert the stream which feeds into the pool by damming it. When the water recedes, they walk around in the mud and pick up the flopping fish by hand. Simple, isn't it?

This fish attains a length of a little over 2 inches.

Exodon paradoxus

This is the most common fish to be found in the Rio Araguaia, which flows through the heart of Brazil. There they occur in such numbers that the Karajá Indians clean their dishes by placing them in the river, where the *Exodon paradoxus* pick them clean. They call them *"miguelinhos"* (little Michaels).

In the aquarium this beautiful fish has the reputation of being a "rough customer," but we have heard that small ones will not bother their tankmates if they grow up with them.

So far we have no reports of their spawning in captivity.

Corydoras myersi

This Catfish was known for quite a while as *C. rabauti,* a name which still persists among some fanciers. He is characterized by a straight line which runs from the top of his head along his back to his tail. He is distinguished from the *C. arcuatus* (page 6) by the fact that this line ends at the top of the head, rather than bending down through the eye to the chin.

We know of only one aquarist, Fred Corwin, who has bred this fish successfully. We were privileged to watch this spawning once at his home. The female picked up the sperm in her mouth and swam toward the surface. Here she pushed her mouth against the glass side of the aquarium to deposit the sperm. At the same time she released three or four eggs, which she held between her ventral fins. Then she pushed these against the glass, where she had deposited the sperm.

The youngsters were a surprise: the rear half of their bodies was bright green, and the front half bright red!

Puntius everetti

This is the well-known and popular "Clown Barb," from Malacca, Singapore and Borneo. He has only one drawback: he is one of the big fellows, attaining a length of about 6 inches.

The color of his sides is a golden yellow, and the dark spots are green. His fins are red, making him a very attractive fish. Usually 1- to 2-inch specimens are sold by dealers. There is very little difference in sexes, except that the female becomes heavier at spawning time and the colors of the male become deeper.

Breeding is easily accomplished in large aquaria, and the young are easily raised.

Phalloceros caudomaculatus var. reticulatus

This is a long name for such a little fish. The original fish is a non-descript fellow, with a spot on the sides at about the middle of the body. We scarcely ever saw it, because the lack of colors kept collectors from shipping it when they could get a better price for highly-colored fishes. When this color variety was discovered and developed, it achieved a moderate popularity and we now find it in fairly good supply.

One cannot fail to identify the males (lower fish). The gonopodium, which is prominent in most livebearing fishes, is quite long in this species. They are very peaceful and stand up well under a lot of abuse. The aquarist who wants to get away from the usual run of livebearers would do well to keep this one.

Carnegiella marthae

This very attractive Hatchet Fish was named after two ladies. The generic name *Carnegiella* is for Miss Margaret Carnegie, and the specific name *marthae* for Martha Ruth Myers, the wife of Dr. George S. Myers, one of our leading ichthyologists. This species of Hatchet Fish is distinguished by his small size (the one pictured is about as big as they grow), and his dark pectoral fins. The Hatchet Fishes are a bit delicate as a rule, but this one is probably the easiest species to keep.

The bizarre shape of these fish makes them a never-ending source of attraction. They are usually found near the surface, and they consequently make good fill-ins in a tank where the fishes tend to stay near the middle or the bottom. Because they are very skillful jumpers, however, the tank in which they are placed must be kept covered. They doubtless acquired their jumping habit in their native haunts, far up the tributaries of the Amazon.

Oryzias javanicus

One thing you will notice immediately in the picture is the extreme transparency of the fish. Even the small bones joining the vertebrae can be seen plainly, thanks to the perfect focussing of the camera.

This is a small, peaceful fish, who gets along well with his neighbors. He is easy to keep and eats any food.

The female expels the eggs in a bunch. They hang from her vent until brushed off.

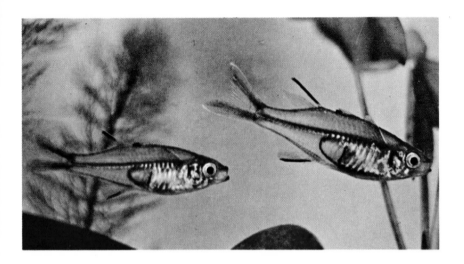

Telmatherina ladigesi

Here is a beautiful aquarium fish who unfortunately is still among the rarities. He has the unusual feature of having two distinct dorsal fins.

He comes from the island of Celebes, Indonesia.

The colors are predominantly silver and yellow. The body is a lemon to golden yellow, and the tip of the first dorsal is black. In the female, the first ray of the dorsal and anal fins is black. In the male, these rays become elongated, and several rays become black. There is a thin blue line which runs the length of the body in both sexes.

This fish has a very shy nature, and needs a well-planted aquarium. If the aquarium is sparsely planted, it drives the fish frantic with fear, and they are very likely to injure themselves by dashing against the glass sides.

Tetraodon schoutedeni

(Above) This comical little fellow is always sure of an audience. Common as the Blowfish is in local marine waters in the summer (see page 64), we must go to Indonesia to find him in fresh waters. He lives well in captivity, and seems to stay healthy and happy for a long time. Another popular freshwater variety is *T. somphongsi* from Thailand, pictured below.

Tetraodon somphongsi

Brachydanio albolineatus

Few aquarium fishes have attained the popularity of the Pearl Danio. They are active, colorful, hardy, and always ready for any food which is offered to them.

A friend who was starting an aquarium once asked us to bring him an egglayer which would be easy to breed. We got him a pair of these, and when we took them out of the cardboard container were surprised to find that they had dropped about twenty eggs there. The eggs were fertile, and after we had raised them to a length of about an inch, our friend got a lot more fish than he had asked for.

There is also a golden color variety of this fish, known as the Gold Danio. Hybridization between the *Brachydanio* species is not difficult, but the offspring are usually sterile.

Chanda buruensis

This is a similar fish to the *Chanda ranga* (page 100), but a bit longer, not quite as transparent, and without the attractive blue edging on the dorsal and anal fins. He is a bit larger, however, attaining a length of a bit over two inches.

It may be noticed that although his body is glassy-transparent, the internal organs are enclosed in a sac which does not permit us to look at them.

This fish has bred in captivity, and in the same manner as the *Chanda ranga*. He requires living foods, and will refuse any other unless faced with starvation.

Gobiochromis tinanti

A look at this fish would hardly identify it as a Cichlid. With its big head and thick, rubbery lips it certainly resembles the marine Gobies, as the name indicates. It comes from the Belgian Congo, like so many other interesting fishes.

A half-dozen or so of these fish in an aquarium of their own is an amusing sight. They are as playful as puppies. One will get on a prominent spot, such as the top of a rock. As soon as the others see him up there, they will do all they can to try to get him off. This game sometimes continues for hours.

Although we had some for quite a while, they never showed any signs of wanting to pair off and spawn.

Cheirodon species

It is difficult to believe that the fish shown here is of the same genus as the gorgeous *Cheirodon axelrodi* (page 22). A fish taxonomist knows better than most people that "you can't tell a book by its cover."

There are many fishes which, because of their lack of color, are never shipped. Still, a closer study of them might disclose some very interesting habits which might more than make up for their lack of color. Collectors consider that a fish does not have a commercial value unless it is colorful, and in most cases they are right, but the serious student of fishes is deprived of many interesting species because of this.

Xiphophorus maculatus (Black Wag Tuxedo)

The Black Wag Tuxedo Platy is one of the developments which succeeded the Black Wag Platy. The two females shown here represent two color varieties, one with a gold back and the other with a red back. Another attractive feature which can be plainly seen in the fish at the left is the black lips. No doubt an all-black fish like the Black Molly will be produced eventually by selective breeding. The original Black Platy had the white belly fairly well bred out, but it has reappeared in this strain; then again, the old strain had no black fins. Here is a real job for a patient breeder.

Glossary

ALBINISM — Black pigmentation almost completely lacking or greatly toned down, but not complete absence of color cells. For instance, where there is a bright blue in the normal fish, the albino shows a light green; red markings become light pink; and where the body is just silvery, it becomes a creamy yellow. Albino fishes are readily recognized by their red eyes. Also see MELANISM and XANTHISM.

ANABANTID — Members of a family of fishes (*Anabantidae*) who obtain oxygen from the atmosphere by means of an auxiliary organ called a labyrinth, as well as by means of gills. Both means of obtaining oxygen must be available. These fish are usually better able to stand crowding or foul water than most fish. Common examples are *Bettas* and Gouramies.

"BARBS" or "BARBUS" — Egg-laying fish with barbels (whisker-like) on their upper lips, such as the *Puntius* family.

BREEDING — See four classifications: BUBBLE-NEST BUILDERS, EGGLAYERS, LIVE-BEARERS, MOUTHBREEDERS.

BUBBLE-NEST BUILDERS — Those fishes who build a floating nest of bubbles in which to deposit their spawn. Examples are Siamese Fighting Fish (*Betta splendens*) and the Gouramies.

CICHLIDS — Of *Cichlidae* family. They are the tropical counterpart of our Sunfishes. Cichlids take about a year or more to mature. They lay adhesive eggs in definite confined area, and the parents take excellent care of their eggs and fry.

CHARACINS — Belong to the family *Characidae,* usually referred to as "tetras." See TETRA.

CLASSIFICATION — See NOMENCLATURE.

DANIO — Minnow-like members of a group of egg-scattering fishes related to *Rasboras.* They usually have barbels. They are active swimmers, not shy, like open water, and are omnivorous.

"DWARF CICHLIDS" — Special group of small Cichlids, under 3 inches in length and with magnificent colors. See CICHLIDS.

EGGLAYERS — Those fishes who fertilize their eggs externally (usually). There are several types of egglaying fishes: (1) the Cichlid types, whose eggs are adhesive, who lay eggs in a definite confined area, and who as parents take care of their fry until they can fend for themselves; and (2) the Tetra or Characin types, who lay scattered eggs, who fertilize them haphazardly, and may eat their own eggs or fry.

FRY — Baby fish just hatched.

GENUS — First name of fish is its genus (or fish family) name. A *genus* is a group of fish who are structurally related.

GONOPODIUM — The long, pointed fin with which the male livebearer transmits his sperm into the body of the female, thereby making it possible for her to carry her young until they are born.

GOURAMI — A term adopted by aquarists to describe nearly every bubble-nest builder except the Siamese Fighting Fish. It has no scientific basis. See BREEDING and ANABANTID.

KILLIFISHES (African) — See PANCHAX.

LABYRINTH — See ANABANTID.

LIVE-BEARERS — Those fishes who deliver their young alive after internal fertilization, but who give no parental care and may even eat their own fry, once the young are born. To save the young, a breeding trap is used.

MELANISM — Complete blackness in coloring. It is a fairly rare condition, usually cultivated by breeding. Black Mollies are one of few available melanotic fishes. Other color varieties such as reds, golds, etc., have been developed, and they all have the same scientific names as the wild varieties of the fish. Also see ALBINISM and XANTHISM.

MOUTHBREEDERS — Those fishes who lay their eggs in special nests, like some Cichlids and Anabantids. Once breeding has been accomplished, one of the parents (usually the male) will pick up the eggs in his mouth and incubate them until they hatch and until the young are able to fend for themselves.

NOMENCLATURE — Fishes, like all animals, have their place in the entire evolutionary development of living things. According to present day *Rules for Zoological Nomenclature,* a binomial system has been arranged. The rules state that the first name of the fish will be the *genus* name, the second part of the name is the *species,* and the third part (if there is a third part) will be the *subspecies* name. For example, the fish *Corydoras melanistius brevirostris* belongs to the genus *Corydoras,* of which there are over a dozen members known to aquarists. He is a subspecies of the species *melanistius,* and the subspecies has been called *brevirostris.* If you think of the names in terms of human names, John Smith as a fish would be Smith John, since he is first a Smith and belongs to that family; he is differentiated from the other members of the family by the name John. If his father's name were also John Smith, he would be Smith John Junior.

PANCHAX — All killifishes of Africa were at one time placed in the genus *Panchax.* This genus is now split up into many other genera (such as *Aphyosemion, Aplocheilus* — from Asia, etc.). Aquarists still commonly talk of any killifish as a *Panchax.*

RIVULUS FISHES — Genus of fish from South America (closely related to killies and minnows of North America); includes the South American killifishes. Most have a typical eye-spot in area between rear edge of the dorsal and the tail fin (caudal peduncle) which is referred to as the "Rivulus spot."

SPECIES — Second part of fish's name. A species of fish (subdivision of a genus) possesses in common one or more distinguishing characteristics; it is a distinct kind; fish of a species do or may interbreed.

SUBSPECIES — If a fish is a subspecies, it will be given a third name. A subspecies is the lowest category recognized in classification, and is a group of fish with more or less unstable distinguishing characteristics. A large group from a particular geographical area may be given a subspecies name.

TETRA — Contraction for *Tetragonopterus* (or *Tetragonopetridae*), a group of fishes usually possessing a dorsal fin and an adipose fin. They lay scattered eggs, and parents eat or give little care to the eggs and fry. These fishes are technically called Characins. See CHARACINS.

XANTHISM — Complete golden color, like Golden Mollie. Also see MELANISM and ALBINISM.

Index

CREDITS

All photographs in this book were taken by G. J. M. Timmerman (*Tropical Fish Hobbyist* Magazine) except for those Aquaphotos by Gene Wolfsheimer on pages 1, 4, 8, 9, 12 (top), 16, 36, 37, 56, 60, 61, 64, 65, 68, 69, 73, 84, 89 (top), 92, 96, 97, 100, 101, 104, 105, 107, 112 (bottom) ; photos by Mervin Roberts appear on pages 121 and 125 ; photos by Harald Schultz appear on pages 19, 70, 83 (bottom), 91, 95, 132, 134 and 135 ; photo by Laurence Perkins appears on page 81 ; photo by Hugo Walter appears on page 54 ; photos by Herbert R. Axelrod appear on pages 6 (top), 10, 14, 15, 17, 23 (bottom), 27 (bottom), 31, 34 (top), 38, 42, 47, 51 (bottom), 55, 62, 63, 66, 67, 71, 74, 87, 90, 102, 111, 118, 119, 120, 122, 123, 126, 127, 129, 131, 133, 137, 138, 140, 142, 144, 147, 148, 150, 152, 153, 154 and 155.